A. Live the New Life

Christt the Center NASB

2 Corinthians 5:17

Therefore if anyone is in Christ, he is a new creature; the old things passed away; behold, new things have come.

2 Corinthians 5:17

A-1   Live the New Life

Christ the Center NASB

Galatians 2:20

I have been crucified with Christ; and it is no longer I who live, but Christ lives in me; and the life which I now live in the flesh I live by faith in the Son of God, who loved me and gave Himself up for me.

Galatians 2:20

A-2   Live the New Life

Obedience to Christ NASB

Romans 12:1

Therefore I urge you, brethren, by the mercies of God, to present your bodies a living and holy sacrifice, acceptable to God, which is your spiritual service of worship.

Romans 12:1

A-3   Live the New Life

Obedience to Christ NASB

John 14:21

He who has My commandments and keeps them is the one who loves Me; and he who loves Me will be loved by My Father, and I will love him and will disclose Myself to him.

John 14:21

A-4   Live the New Life

God's Word NASB

2 Timothy 3:16

All Scripture is inspired by God and profitable for teaching, for reproof, for correction, for training in righteousness.

2 Timothy 3:16

A-5   Live the New Life

God's Word NASB

Joshua 1:8

This book of the law shall not depart from your mouth, but you shall meditate on it day and night, so that you may be careful to do according to all that is written in it; for then you will make your way prosperous, and then you will have success.

Joshua 1:8

A-6   Live the New Life

Prayer NASB

John 15:7

If you abide in Me, and My words abide in you, ask whatever you wish, and it will be done for you.

John 15:7

A-7   Live the New Life

Prayer NASB

Philippians 4:6-7

Be anxious for nothing, but in everything by prayer and supplication with thanksgiving let your requests be made known to God. And the peace of God, which surpasses all comprehension, will guard your hearts and your minds in Christ Jesus.

Philippians 4:6-7

A-8   Live the New Life

A. Live the New Life

A. Live the New Life

Christt the Center   NKJV
Galatians 2:20

I have been crucified with Christ; it is no longer I who live, but Christ lives in me; and the life which I now live in the flesh I live by faith in the Son of God, who loved me and gave Himself for me.

Galatians 2:20

A-2   Live the New Life

Christ the Center   NKJV
2 Corinthians 5:17

Therefore, if anyone is in Christ, he is a new creation; old things have passed away; behold, all things have become new.

2 Corinthians 5:17

A-1   Live the New Life

Obedience to Christ   NKJV
John 14:21

He who has My commandments and keeps them, it is he who loves Me. And he who loves Me will be loved by My Father, and I will love him and manifest Myself to him.

John 14:21

A-4   Live the New Life

Obedience to Christ   NKJV
Romans 12:1

I beseech you therefore, brethren, by the mercies of God, that you present your bodies a living sacrifice, holy, acceptable to God, which is your reasonable service.

Romans 12:1

A-3   Live the New Life

God's Word   NKJV
Joshua 1:8

This Book of the Law shall not depart from your mouth, but you shall meditate in it day and night, that you may observe to do according to all that is written in it. For then you will make your way prosperous, and then you will have good success.

Joshua 1:8

A-6   Live the New Life

God's Word   NKJV
2 Timothy 3:16

All Scripture is given by inspiration of God, and is profitable for doctrine, for reproof, for correction, for instruction in righteousness.

2 Timothy 3:16

A-5   Live the New Life

Prayer   NKJV
Philippians 4:6-7

Be anxious for nothing, but in everything by prayer and supplication, with thanksgiving, let your requests be made known to God; and the peace of God, which surpasses all understanding, will guard your hearts and minds through Christ Jesus.

Philippians 4:6-7

A-8   Live the New Life

Prayer   NKJV
John 15:7

If you abide in Me, and My words abide in you, you will ask what you desire, and it shall be done for you.

John 15:7

A-7   Live the New Life

A. Live the New Life

A. Live the New Life

Christ the Center   ESV

2 Corinthians 5:17

Therefore, if anyone is in Christ, he is a new creation. The old has passed away; behold, the new has come.

2 Corinthians 5:17

A-1   Live the New Life

Christ the Center   ESV

Galatians 2:20

I have been crucified with Christ. It is no longer I who live, but Christ who lives in me. And the life I now live in the flesh I live by faith in the Son of God, who loved me and gave himself for me.

Galatians 2:20

A-2   Live the New Life

Obedience to Christ   ESV

Romans 12:1

I appeal to you therefore, brothers, by the mercies of God, to present your bodies as a living sacrifice, holy and acceptable to God, which is your spiritual worship.

Romans 12:1

A-3   Live the New Life

Obedience to Christ   ESV

John 14:21

Whoever has my commandments and keeps them, he it is who loves me. And he who loves me will be loved by my Father, and I will love him and manifest myself to him.

John 14:21

A-4   Live the New Life

God's Word   ESV

2 Timothy 3:16

All Scripture is breathed out by God and profitable for teaching, for reproof, for correction, and for training in righteousness.

2 Timothy 3:16

A-5   Live the New Life

God's Word   ESV

Joshua 1:8

This Book of the Law shall not depart from your mouth, but you shall meditate on it day and night, so that you may be careful to do according to all that is written in it. For then you will make your way prosperous, and then you will have good success.

Joshua 1:8

A-6   Live the New Life

Prayer   ESV

John 15:7

If you abide in me, and my words abide in you, ask whatever you wish, and it will be done for you.

John 15:7

A-7   Live the New Life

Prayer   ESV

Philippians 4:6-7

Do not be anxious about anything, but in everything by prayer and supplication with thanksgiving let your requests be made known to God. And the peace of God, which surpasses all understanding, will guard your hearts and your minds in Christ Jesus.

Philippians 4:6-7

A-8   Live the New Life

A. Live the New Life

A. Live the New Life

Christic the Center

Christ the Center   KJV

Galatians 2:20

I am crucified with Christ: nevertheless I live; yet not I, but Christ liveth in me: and the life which I now live in the flesh I live by the faith of the Son of God, who loved me, and gave himself for me.

Galatians 2:20

A-2   *Live the New Life*

Christ the Center   KJV

2 Corinthians 5:17

Therefore if any man be in Christ, he is a new creature: old things are passed away; behold, all things are become new.

2 Corinthians 5:17

A-1   *Live the New Life*

Obedience to Christ   KJV

John 14:21

He that hath my commandments, and keepeth them, he it is that loveth me: and he that loveth me shall be loved of my Father, and I will love him, and will manifest myself to him.

John 14:21

A-4   *Live the New Life*

Obedience to Christ   KJV

Romans 12:1

I beseech you therefore, brethren, by the mercies of God, that ye present your bodies a living sacrifice, holy, acceptable unto God, which is your reasonable service.

Romans 12:1

A-3   *Live the New Life*

God's Word   KJV

Joshua 1:8

This book of the law shall not depart out of thy mouth; but thou shalt meditate therein day and night, that thou mayest observe to do according to all that is written therein: for then thou shalt make thy way prosperous, and then thou shalt have good success.

Joshua 1:8

A-6   *Live the New Life*

God's Word   KJV

2 Timothy 3:16

All scripture is given by inspiration of God, and is profitable for doctrine, for reproof, for correction, for instruction in righteousness.

2 Timothy 3:16

A-5   *Live the New Life*

Prayer   KJV

Philippians 4:6-7

Be careful for nothing; but in everything by prayer and supplication with thanksgiving let your requests be made known unto God. And the peace of God, which passeth all understanding, shall keep your hearts and minds through Christ Jesus.

Philippians 4:6-7

A-8   *Live the New Life*

Prayer   KJV

John 15:7

If ye abide in me, and my words abide in you, ye shall ask what ye will, and it shall be done unto you.

John 15:7

A-7   *Live the New Life*

A. Live the New Life

A. Live the New Life

Christic the Center

Christ the Center — NRSV

2 Corinthians 5:17

So if anyone is in Christ, there is a new creation: everything old has passed away; see, everything has become new!

2 Corinthians 5:17

A-1   *Live the New Life*

Christ the Center — NRSV

Galatians 2:20

And it is no longer I who live, but it is Christ who lives in me. And the life I now live in the flesh I live by faith in the Son of God, who loved me and gave himself for me.

Galatians 2:20

A-2   *Live the New Life*

Obedience to Christ — NRSV

Romans 12:1

I appeal to you therefore, brothers and sisters, by the mercies of God, to present your bodies as a living sacrifice, holy and acceptable to God, which is your spiritual worship.

Romans 12:1

A-3   *Live the New Life*

Obedience to Christ — NRSV

John 14:21

They who have my commandments and keep them are those who love me; and those who love me will be loved by my Father, and I will love them and reveal myself to them.

John 14:21

A-4   *Live the New Life*

God's Word — NRSV

2 Timothy 3:16

All scripture is inspired by God and is useful for teaching, for reproof, for correction, and for training in righteousness.

2 Timothy 3:16

A-5   *Live the New Life*

God's Word — NRSV

Joshua 1:8

This book of the law shall not depart out of your mouth; you shall meditate on it day and night, so that you may be careful to act in accordance with all that is written in it. For then you shall make your way prosperous, and then you shall be successful.

Joshua 1:8

A-6   *Live the New Life*

Prayer — NRSV

John 15:7

If you abide in me, and my words abide in you, ask for whatever you wish, and it will be done for you.

John 15:7

A-7   *Live the New Life*

Prayer — NRSV

Philippians 4:6-7

Do not worry about anything, but in everything by prayer and supplication with thanksgiving let your requests be made known to God. And the peace of God, which surpasses all understanding, will guard your hearts and your minds in Christ Jesus.

Philippians 4:6-7

A-8   *Live the New Life*

A. Live the New Life

A. Live the New Life

Christic the Center

Christ the Center NLT

Galatians 2:20

I myself no longer live, but Christ lives in me. So I live my life in this earthly body by trusting in the Son of God, who loved me and gave himself for me.

Galatians 2:20

A-2 Live the New Life

Christ the Center NLT

2 Corinthians 5:17

What this means is that those who become Christians become new persons. They are not the same anymore, for the old life is gone. A new life has begun!

2 Corinthians 5:17

A-1 Live the New Life

Obedience to Christ NLT

John 14:21

Those who obey my commandments are the ones who love me. And because they love me, my Father will love them, and I will love them. And I will reveal myself to each one of them.

John 14:21

A-4 Live the New Life

Obedience to Christ NLT

Romans 12:1

And so, dear brothers and sisters, I plead with you to give your bodies to God. Let them be a living and holy sacrifice — the kind he will accept. When you think of what he has done for you, is this too much to ask?

Romans 12:1

A-3 Live the New Life

God's Word NLT

Joshua 1:8

Study this Book of the Law continually. Meditate on it day and night so you may be sure to obey all that is written in it. Only then will you succeed.

Joshua 1:8

A-6 Live the New Life

God's Word NLT

2 Timothy 3:16

All Scripture is inspired by God and is useful to teach us what is true and to make us realize what is wrong in our lives. It straightens us out and teaches us to do what is right.

2 Timothy 3:16

A-5 Live the New Life

Prayer NLT

Philippians 4:6-7

Don't worry about anything; instead, pray about everything. Tell God what you need, and thank him for all he has done. If you do this, you will experience God's peace, which is far more wonderful than the human mind can understand. His peace will guard your hearts and minds as you live in Christ Jesus.

Philippians 4:6-7

A-8 Live the New Life

Prayer NLT

John 15:7

But if you stay joined to me and my words remain in you, you may ask any request you like, and it will be granted!

John 15:7

A-7 Live the New Life

A. Live the New Life

A. Live the New Life

Fellowship   NIV
1 John 1:3

We proclaim to you what we have seen and heard, so that you also may have fellowship with us. And our fellowship is with the Father and with his Son, Jesus Christ.

1 John 1:3

A-9 Live the New Life

Fellowship   NIV
Hebrews 10:24-25

And let us consider how we may spur one another on toward love and good deeds, not giving up meeting together, as some are in the habit of doing, but encouraging one another — and all the more as you see the Day approaching.

Hebrews 10:24-25

A-10 Live the New Life

Witnessing   NIV
Matthew 4:19

"Come, follow me," Jesus said, "and I will send you out to fish for people."

Matthew 4:19

A-11 Live the New Life

Witnessing   NIV
Romans 1:16

For I am not ashamed of the gospel, because it is the power of God that brings salvation to everyone who believes: first to the Jew, then to the Gentile.

Romans 1:16

A-12 Live the New Life

TOPICAL MEMORY SYSTEM
A. Live the New Life
- Christ the Center — 2 Corinthians 5:17; Galatians 2:20
- Obedience to Christ — Romans 12:1; John 14:21
- God's Word — 2 Timothy 3:16; Joshua 1:8
- Prayer — John 15:7; Philippians 4:6-7
- Fellowship — 1 John 1:3; Hebrews 10:24-25
- Witnessing — Matthew 4:19; Romans 1:16

B. Proclaim Christ
- All Have Sinned — Romans 3:23; Isaiah 53:6
- Sin's Penalty — Romans 6:23; Hebrews 9:27
- Christ Paid the Penalty — Romans 5:8; 1 Peter 3:18
- Salvation Not by Works — Ephesians 2:8-9; Titus 3:5
- Must Receive Christ — John 1:12; Revelation 3:20
- Assurance of Salvation — 1 John 5:13; John 5:24

C. Rely on God's Resources
- His Spirit — 1 Corinthians 3:16; 1 Corinthians 2:12
- His Strength — Isaiah 41:10; Philippians 4:13
- His Faithfulness — Lamentations 3:22-23; Numbers 23:19
- His Peace — Isaiah 26:3; 1 Peter 5:7
- His Provision — Romans 8:32; Philippians 4:19
- His Help in Temptation — Hebrews 2:18; Psalm 119:9, 11

D. Be Christ's Disciple
- Put Christ First — Matthew 6:33; Luke 9:23
- Separate from the World — 1 John 2:15-16; Romans 12:2
- Be Steadfast — 1 Corinthians 15:58; Hebrews 12:3
- Serve Others — Mark 10:45; 2 Corinthians 4:5
- Give Generously — Proverbs 3:9-10; 2 Corinthians 9:6-7
- Develop World Vision — Acts 1:8; Matthew 28:19-20

TOPICAL MEMORY SYSTEM (cont)
E. Grow in Christlikeness
- Love — John 13:34-35; 1 John 3:18
- Humility — Philippians 2:3-4; 1 Peter 5:5-6
- Purity — Ephesians 5:3; 1 Peter 2:11
- Honesty — Leviticus 19:11; Acts 24:16
- Faith — Hebrews 11:6; Romans 4:20-21
- Good Works — Galatians 6:9-10; Matthew 5:16

This Pack Belongs To

Name _____

Address _____

_____

Phone _____

If found, please return to above address.

A. Live the New Life

A. Live the New Life

Fellowship   MSG

Hebrews 10:24-25

Let's see how inventive we can be in encour-aging love and helping out, not avoiding worshiping together as some do but spurring each other on, especially as we see the big Day approaching.

Hebrews 10:24-25

A-10   Live the New Life

Witnessing   MSG

Romans 1:16

It's news I'm most proud to proclaim, this extraordinary Message of God's powerful plan to rescue everyone who trusts him, starting with Jews and then right on to everyone else!

Romans 1:16

A-12   Live the New Life

Fellowship   MSG

1 John 1:3

We saw it, we heard it, and now we're telling you so you can experience it along with us, this experience of communion with the Father and his Son, Jesus Christ.

1 John 1:3

A-9   Live the New Life

Witnessing   MSG

Matthew 4:19

Jesus said to them, "Come with me. I'll make a new kind of fisherman out of you. I'll show you how to catch men and women instead of perch and bass."

Matthew 4:19

A-11   Live the New Life

A. Live the New Life

A. Live the New Life

Fellowship NASB
1 John 1:3

What we have seen and heard we proclaim to you also, so that you too may have fellowship with us; and indeed our fellowship is with the Father, and with His Son Jesus Christ.

1 John 1:3

A-9   Live the New Life

Fellowship NASB
Hebrews 10:24-25

And let us consider how to stimulate one another to love and good deeds, not forsaking our own assembling together, as is the habit of some, but encouraging one another; and all the more as you see the day drawing near.

Hebrews 10:24-25

A-10   Live the New Life

Witnessing NASB
Matthew 4:19

And He said to them, "Follow Me, and I will make you fishers of men."

Matthew 4:19

A-11   Live the New Life

Witnessing NASB
Romans 1:16

For I am not ashamed of the gospel, for it is the power of God for salvation to everyone who believes, to the Jew first and also to the Greek.

Romans 1:16

A-12   Live the New Life

A. Live the New Life

A. Live the New Life

Fellowship   NKJV

Hebrews 10:24-25

And let us consider one another in order to stir up love and good works, not forsaking the assembling of ourselves together, as is the manner of some, but exhorting one another, and so much the more as you see the Day approaching.

Hebrews 10:24-25

A-10   Live the New Life

Fellowship   NKJV

1 John 1:3

That which we have seen and heard we declare to you, that you may also have fellowship with us; and truly our fellowship is with the Father and with his Son Jesus Christ.

1 John 1:3

A-9   Live the New Life

Witnessing   NKJV

Romans 1:16

For I am not ashamed of the gospel of Christ, for it is the power of God to salvation for everyone who believes, for the Jew first and also for the Greek.

Romans 1:16

A-12   Live the New Life

Witnessing   NKJV

Matthew 4:19

And He said to them, "Follow Me, and I will make you fishers of men."

Matthew 4:19

A-11   Live the New Life

A. Live the New Life

A. Live the New Life

Fellowship ESV

1 John 1:3

That which we have seen and heard we proclaim also to you, so that you too may have fellowship with us; and indeed our fellowship is with the Father and with his Son Jesus Christ

1 John 1:3

A-9   *Live the New Life*

Fellowship ESV

Hebrews 10:24-25

And let us consider how to stir up one another to love and good works, not neglecting to meet together, as is the habit of some, but encouraging one another, and all the more as you see the Day drawing near.

Hebrews 10:24-25

A-10   *Live the New Life*

Witnessing ESV

Matthew 4:19

And he said to them, "Follow me, and I will make you fishers of men."

Matthew 4:19

A-11   *Live the New Life*

Witnessing ESV

Romans 1:16

For I am not ashamed of the gospel, for it is the power of God for salvation to everyone who believes, to the Jew first and also to the Greek.

Romans 1:16

A-12   *Live the New Life*

A. Live the New Life

A. Live the New Life

Fellowship   KJV
Hebrews 10:24-25

And let us consider one another to provoke unto love and to good works: not forsaking the assembling of ourselves together, as the manner of some is; but exhorting one another: and so much the more as ye see the day approaching.

Hebrews 10:24-25

A-10   Live the New Life

Fellowship   KJV
1 John 1:3

That which we have seen and heard declare we unto you, that ye also may have fellowship with us: and truly our fellowship is with the Father, and with his Son Jesus Christ.

1 John 1:3

A-9   Live the New Life

Witnessing   KJV
Romans 1:16

For I am not ashamed of the gospel of Christ: for it is the power of God unto salvation to every one that believeth; to the Jew first, and also to the Greek.

Romans 1:16

A-12   Live the New Life

Witnessing   KJV
Matthew 4:19

And he saith unto them, Follow Me, and I will make you fishers of men.

Matthew 4:19

A-11   Live the New Life

A. Live the New Life

A. Live the New Life

Fellowship
NRSV

1 John 1:3

We declare to you what we have seen and heard so that you also may have fellowship with us; and truly our fellowship is with the Father and with his Son Jesus Christ.

1 John 1:3

A-9   Live the New Life

Witnessing
NRSV

Matthew 4:19

And he said to them, "Follow me, and I will make you fish for people."

Matthew 4:19

A-11   Live the New Life

Fellowship
NRSV

Hebrews 10:24-25

And let us consider how to provoke one another to love and good deeds, not neglecting to meet together, as is the habit of some, but encouraging one another, and all the more as you see the Day approaching.

Hebrews 10:24-25

A-10   Live the New Life

Witnessing
NRSV

Romans 1:16

For I am not ashamed of the gospel; it is the power of God for salvation to everyone who has faith, to the Jew first and also to the Greek.

Romans 1:16

A-12   Live the New Life

A. Live the New Life

A. Live the New Life

Fellowship
NLT

Hebrews 10:24-25

Think of ways to encourage one another to outbursts of love and good deeds. And let us not neglect our meeting together, as some people do, but encourage and warn each other, especially now that the day of his coming back again is drawing near.

Hebrews 10:24-25

A-10   Live the New Life

Fellowship
NLT

1 John 1:3

We are telling you about what we ourselves have actually seen and heard, so that you may have fellowship with us. And our fellowship is with the Father and with his Son, Jesus Christ.

1 John 1:3

A-9   Live the New Life

Witnessing
NLT

Romans 1:16

For I am not ashamed of this Good News about Christ. It is the power of God at work, saving everyone who believes — Jews first and also Gentiles.

Romans 1:16

A-12   Live the New Life

Witnessing
NLT

Matthew 4:19

Jesus called out to them, "Come, be my disciples, and I will show you how to fish for people!"

Matthew 4:19

A-11   Live the New Life

B. Proclaim Christ

B. Proclaim Christ

All Have Sinned
NIV

Romans 3:23

For all have sinned and fall short of the glory of God.

Romans 3:23

All Have Sinned
NIV

Isaiah 53:6

We all, like sheep, have gone astray, each of us has turned to our own way; and the LORD has laid on him the iniquity of us all.

Isaiah 53:6

Sin's Penalty
NIV

Romans 6:23

For the wages of sin is death, but the gift of God is eternal life in Christ Jesus our Lord.

Romans 6:23

Sin's Penalty
NIV

Hebrews 9:27

Just as people are destined to die once, and after that to face judgment.

Hebrews 9:27

Christ Paid the Penalty
NIV

Romans 5:8

But God demonstrates his own love for us in this: While we were still sinners, Christ died for us.

Romans 5:8

Christ Paid the Penalty
NIV

1 Peter 3:18

For Christ suffered once for sins, the righteous for the unrighteous, to bring you to God. He was put to death in the body but made alive in the Spirit.

1 Peter 3:18

Salvation Not by Works
NIV

Ephesians 2:8-9

For it is by grace you have been saved, through faith — and this not from yourselves, it is the gift of God — not by works, so that no one can boast.

Ephesians 2:8-9

Salvation Not by Works
NIV

Titus 3:5

He saved us, not because of righteous things we had done, but because of his mercy. He saved us through the washing of rebirth and renewal by the Holy Spirit.

Titus 3:5

B. Proclaim Christ

B. Proclaim Christ

All Have Sinned — MSG

Isaiah 53:6

We're all like sheep who've wandered off and gotten lost. We've all done our own thing, gone our own way. And GOD has piled all our sins, everything we've done wrong, on him.

Isaiah 53:6

B-2   Proclaim Christ

All Have Sinned — MSG

Romans 3:23

Since we've compiled this long and sorry record as sinners (both us and them) and proved that we are utterly incapable of living the glorious lives God wills for us.

Romans 3:23

B-1   Proclaim Christ

Sin's Penalty — MSG

Hebrews 9:27

Everyone has to die once, then face the consequences.

Hebrews 9:27

B-4   Proclaim Christ

Sin's Penalty — MSG

Romans 6:23

Work hard for sin your whole life and your pension is death. But God's gift is *real life*, eternal life, delivered by Jesus, our Master.

Romans 6:23

B-3   Proclaim Christ

Christ Paid the Penalty — MSG

1 Peter 3:18

That's what Christ did definitively: suffered because of others' sins, the Righteous One for the unrighteous ones. He went through it all — was put to death and then made alive — to bring us to God.

1 Peter 3:18

B-6   Proclaim Christ

Christ Paid the Penalty — MSG

Romans 5:8

But God put his love on the line for us by offering his Son in sacrificial death while we were of no use whatever to him.

Romans 5:8

B-5   Proclaim Christ

Salvation Not by Works — MSG

Titus 3:5

He saved us from all that. It was all his doing; we had nothing to do with it. He gave us a good bath, and we came out of it new people, washed inside and out by the Holy Spirit.

Titus 3:5

B-8   Proclaim Christ

Salvation Not by Works — MSG

Ephesians 2:8-9

Saving is all his idea, and all his work. All we do is trust him enough to let him do it. It's God's gift from start to finish! We don't play the major role. If we did, we'd probably go around bragging that we'd done the whole thing!

Ephesians 2:8-9

B-7   Proclaim Christ

All Have Sinned   NASB

Romans 3:23

For all have sinned and fall short of the glory of God.

Romans 3:23

All Have Sinned   NASB

Isaiah 53:6

All of us like sheep have gone astray, each of us has turned to his own way; but the LORD has caused the iniquity of us all to fall on Him.

Isaiah 53:6

Sin's Penalty   NASB

Romans 6:23

For the wages of sin is death, but the free gift of God is eternal life in Christ Jesus our Lord.

Romans 6:23

Sin's Penalty   NASB

Hebrews 9:27

And inasmuch as it is appointed for men to die once and after this comes judgment.

Hebrews 9:27

Christ Paid the Penalty   NASB

Romans 5:8

But God demonstrates His own love toward us, in that while we were yet sinners, Christ died for us.

Romans 5:8

Christ Paid the Penalty   NASB

1 Peter 3:18

For Christ also died for sins once for all, the just for the unjust, so that He might bring us to God, having been put to death in the flesh, but made alive in the spirit.

1 Peter 3:18

Salvation Not by Works   NASB

Ephesians 2:8-9

For by grace you have been saved through faith; and that not of yourselves, it is the gift of God; not as a result of works, so that no one may boast.

Ephesians 2:8-9

Salvation Not by Works   NASB

Titus 3:5

He saved us, not on the basis of deeds which we have done in righteousness, but according to His mercy, by the washing of regeneration and renewing by the Holy Spirit.

Titus 3:5

B. Proclaim Christ

B. Proclaim Christ

All Have Sinned NKJV
Isaiah 53:6

All we like sheep have gone astray; we have turned, every one, to his own way; and the LORD has laid on Him the iniquity of us all.

Isaiah 53:6

B-2   Proclaim Christ

All Have Sinned NKJV
Romans 3:23

For all have sinned and fall short of the glory of God.

Romans 3:23

B-1   Proclaim Christ

Sin's Penalty NKJV
Hebrews 9:27

And as it is appointed for men to die once, but after this the judgment.

Hebrews 9:27

B-4   Proclaim Christ

Sin's Penalty NKJV
Romans 6:23

For the wages of sin is death, but the gift of God is eternal life in Christ Jesus our Lord.

Romans 6:23

B-3   Proclaim Christ

Christ Paid the Penalty NKJV
1 Peter 3:18

For Christ also suffered once for sins, the just for the unjust, that He might bring us to God, being put to death in the flesh but made alive by the Spirit.

1 Peter 3:18

B-6   Proclaim Christ

Christ Paid the Penalty NKJV
Romans 5:8

But God demonstrates His own love toward us, in that while we were still sinners, Christ died for us.

Romans 5:8

B-5   Proclaim Christ

Salvation Not by Works NKJV
Titus 3:5

Not by works of righteousness which we have done, but according to His mercy He saved us, through the washing of regeneration and renewing of the Holy Spirit.

Titus 3:5

B-8   Proclaim Christ

Salvation Not by Works NKJV
Ephesians 2:8-9

For by grace you have been saved through faith, and that not of yourselves; it is the gift of God, not of works, lest anyone should boast.

Ephesians 2:8-9

B-7   Proclaim Christ

B. Proclaim Christ

B. Proclaim Christ

All Have Sinned ESV

Romans 3:23

For all have sinned and fall short of the glory of God.

Romans 3:23

B-1   *Proclaim Christ*

All Have Sinned ESV

Isaiah 53:6

All we like sheep have gone astray; we have turned every one to his own way; and the Lord has laid on him the iniquity of us all.

Isaiah 53:6

B-2   *Proclaim Christ*

Sin's Penalty ESV

Romans 6:23

For the wages of sin is death, but the free gift of God is eternal life in Christ Jesus our Lord.

Romans 6:23

B-3   *Proclaim Christ*

Sin's Penalty ESV

Hebrews 9:27

And just as it is appointed for man to die once, and after that comes judgment.

Hebrews 9:27

B-4   *Proclaim Christ*

Christ Paid the Penalty ESV

Romans 5:8

But God shows his love for us in that while we were still sinners, Christ died for us.

Romans 5:8

B-5   *Proclaim Christ*

Christ Paid the Penalty ESV

1 Peter 3:18

For Christ also suffered once for sins, the righteous for the unrighteous, that he might bring us to God, being put to death in the flesh but made alive in the spirit.

1 Peter 3:18

B-6   *Proclaim Christ*

Salvation Not by Works ESV

Ephesians 2:8-9

For by grace you have been saved through faith. And this is not your own doing; it is the gift of God, not a result of works, so that no one may boast.

Ephesians 2:8-9

B-7   *Proclaim Christ*

Salvation Not by Works ESV

Titus 3:5

He saved us, not because of works done by us in righteousness, but according to his own mercy, by the washing of regeneration and renewal of the Holy Spirit.

Titus 3:5

B-8   *Proclaim Christ*

B. Proclaim Christ

B. Proclaim Christ

All Have Sinned   KJV

Isaiah 53:6

All we like sheep have gone astray; we have turned every one to his own way; and the LORD hath laid on him the iniquity of us all.

Isaiah 53:6

All Have Sinned   KJV

Romans 3:23

For all have sinned, and come short of the glory of God.

Romans 3:23

Sin's Penalty   KJV

Hebrews 9:27

And as it is appointed unto men once to die, but after this the judgment.

Hebrews 9:27

Sin's Penalty   KJV

Romans 6:23

For the wages of sin is death; but the gift of God is eternal life through Jesus Christ our Lord.

Romans 6:23

Christ Paid the Penalty   KJV

1 Peter 3:18

For Christ also hath once suffered for sins, the just for the unjust, that he might bring us to God, being put to death in the flesh, but quickened by the Spirit.

1 Peter 3:18

Christ Paid the Penalty   KJV

Romans 5:8

But God commendeth his love toward us, in that, while we were yet sinners, Christ died for us.

Romans 5:8

Salvation Not by Works   KJV

Titus 3:5

Not by works of righteousness which we have done, but according to his mercy he saved us, by the washing of regeneration, and renewing of the Holy Ghost.

Titus 3:5

Salvation Not by Works   KJV

Ephesians 2:8-9

For by grace are ye saved through faith; and that not of yourselves: it is the gift of God: Not of works, lest any man should boast.

Ephesians 2:8-9

All Have Sinned · NRSV

Romans 3:23

Since all have sinned and fall short of the glory of God.

Romans 3:23

B-1   *Proclaim Christ*

All Have Sinned · NRSV

Isaiah 53:6

All we like sheep have gone astray; we have all turned to our own way, and the Lord has laid on him the iniquity of us all.

Isaiah 53:6

B-2   *Proclaim Christ*

Sin's Penalty · NRSV

Romans 6:23

For the wages of sin is death, but the free gift of God is eternal life in Christ Jesus our Lord.

Romans 6:23

B-3   *Proclaim Christ*

Sin's Penalty · NRSV

Hebrews 9:27

And just as it is appointed for mortals to die once, and after that the judgment.

Hebrews 9:27

B-4   *Proclaim Christ*

Christ Paid the Penalty · NRSV

Romans 5:8

But God proves his love for us in that while we still were sinners Christ died for us.

Romans 5:8

B-5   *Proclaim Christ*

Christ Paid the Penalty · NRSV

1 Peter 3:18

For Christ also suffered for sins once for all, the righteous for the unrighteous, in order to bring you to God. He was put to death in the flesh, but made alive in the spirit.

1 Peter 3:18

B-6   *Proclaim Christ*

Salvation Not by Works · NRSV

Ephesians 2:8-9

For by grace you have been saved through faith, and this is not your own doing; it is the gift of God — not the result of works, so that no one may boast.

Ephesians 2:8-9

B-7   *Proclaim Christ*

Salvation Not by Works · NRSV

Titus 3:5

He saved us, not because of any works of righteousness that we had done, but according to his mercy, through the water of rebirth and renewal by the Holy Spirit.

Titus 3:5

B-8   *Proclaim Christ*

All Have Sinned   NLT

Isaiah 53:6

All of us have strayed away like sheep. We have left God's paths to follow our own. Yet the LORD laid on him the guilt and sins of us all.

Isaiah 53:6

B-2   Proclaim Christ

All Have Sinned   NLT

Romans 3:23

For all have sinned; all fall short of God's glorious standard.

Romans 3:23

B-1   Proclaim Christ

Sin's Penalty   NLT

Hebrews 9:27

And just as it is destined that each person dies only once and after that comes judgment.

Hebrews 9:27

B-4   Proclaim Christ

Sin's Penalty   NLT

Romans 6:23

For the wages of sin is death, but the free gift of God is eternal life through Christ Jesus our Lord.

Romans 6:23

B-3   Proclaim Christ

Christ Paid the Penalty   NLT

1 Peter 3:18

Christ also suffered when he died for our sins once for all time. He never sinned, but he died for sinners that he might bring us safely home to God. He suffered physical death, but he was raised to life in the Spirit.

1 Peter 3:18

B-6   Proclaim Christ

Christ Paid the Penalty   NLT

Romans 5:8

But God showed his great love for us by sending Christ to die for us while we were still sinners.

Romans 5:8

B-5   Proclaim Christ

Salvation Not by Works   NLT

Titus 3:5

He saved us, not because of the good things we did, but because of his mercy. He washed away our sins and gave us a new life through the Holy Spirit.

Titus 3:5

B-8   Proclaim Christ

Salvation Not by Works   NLT

Ephesians 2:8-9

God saved you by his special favor when you believed. And you can't take credit for this; it is a gift from God. Salvation is not a reward for the good things we have done, so none of us can boast about it.

Ephesians 2:8-9

B-7   Proclaim Christ

B. Proclaim Christ

B. Proclaim Christ

Must Receive Christ   NIV
John 1:12

Yet to all who did receive him, to those who believed in his name, he gave the right to become children of God.

John 1:12

Must Receive Christ   NIV
Revelation 3:20

Here I am! I stand at the door and knock. If anyone hears my voice and opens the door, I will come in and eat with that person, and they with me.

Revelation 3:20

Assurance of Salvation   NIV
1 John 5:13

I write these things to you who believe in the name of the Son of God so that you may know that you have eternal life.

1 John 5:13

Assurance of Salvation   NIV
John 5:24

Very truly I tell you, whoever hears my word and believes him who sent me has eternal life and will not be judged but has crossed over from death to life.

John 5:24

TOPICAL MEMORY SYSTEM
A. Live the New Life
Christ the Center—2 Corinthians 5:17; Galatians 2:20
Obedience to Christ—Romans 12:1; John 14:21
God's Word—2 Timothy 3:16; Joshua 1:8
Prayer—John 15:7; Philippians 4:6-7
Fellowship—1 John 1:3; Hebrews 10:24-25
Witnessing—Matthew 4:19; Romans 1:16
B. Proclaim Christ
All Have Sinned—Romans 3:23; Isaiah 53:6
Sin's Penalty—Romans 6:23; Hebrews 9:27
Christ Paid the Penalty—Romans 5:8; 1 Peter 3:18
Salvation Not by Works—Ephesians 2:8-9; Titus 3:5
Must Receive Christ—John 1:12; Revelation 3:20
Assurance of Salvation—1 John 5:13; John 5:24

C. Rely on God's Resources
His Spirit—1 Corinthians 3:16; 1 Corinthians 2:12
His Strength—Isaiah 41:10; Philippians 4:13
His Faithfulness—Lamentations 3:22-23; Numbers 23:19
His Peace—Isaiah 26:3; 1 Peter 5:7
His Provision—Romans 8:32; Philippians 4:19
His Help in Temptation—Hebrews 2:18; Psalm 119:9, 11
D. Be Christ's Disciple
Put Christ First—Matthew 6:33; Luke 9:23
Separate from the World—1 John 2:15-16; Romans 12:2
Be Steadfast—1 Corinthians 15:58; Hebrews 12:3
Serve Others—Mark 10:45; 2 Corinthians 4:5
Give Generously—Proverbs 3:9-10; 2 Corinthians 9:6-7
Develop World Vision—Acts 1:8; Matthew 28:19-20

TOPICAL MEMORY SYSTEM (cont)
E. Grow in Christlikeness
Love—John 13:34-35; 1 John 3:18
Humility—Philippians 2:3-4; 1 Peter 5:5-6
Purity—Ephesians 5:3; 1 Peter 2:11
Honesty—Leviticus 19:11; Acts 24:16
Faith—Hebrews 11:6; Romans 4:20-21
Good Works—Galatians 6:9-10; Matthew 5:16

This Pack Belongs To

Name _____

Address _____

_____

Phone _____

If found, please return to above address.

B. Proclaim Christ

B. Proclaim Christ

Must Receive Christ   MSG
Revelation 3:20

Look at me. I stand at the door. I knock. If you hear me call and open the door, I'll come right in and sit down to supper with you.

Revelation 3:20

B-10   Proclaim Christ

Must Receive Christ   MSG
John 1:12

But whoever did want him, who believed he was who he claimed and would do what he said, he made to be their true selves, their child-of-God selves.

John 1:12

B-9   Proclaim Christ

Assurance of Salvation   MSG
John 5:24

It's urgent that you listen carefully to this: Anyone here who believes what I am saying right now and aligns himself with the Father, who has in fact put me in charge, has at this very moment the real, lasting life and is no longer condemned to be an outsider. This person has taken a giant step from the world of the dead to the world of the living.

John 5:24

B-12   Proclaim Christ

Assurance of Salvation   MSG
1 John 5:13

My purpose in writing is simply this: that you who believe in God's Son will know beyond the shadow of a doubt that you have eternal life, the reality and not the illusion.

1 John 5:13

B-11   Proclaim Christ

B. Proclaim Christ

B. Proclaim Christ

Must Receive Christ   NASB

John 1:12

But as many as received Him, to them He gave the right to become children of God, even to those who believe in His name.

John 1:12

B-9   Proclaim Christ

Must Receive Christ   NASB

Revelation 3:20

Behold, I stand at the door and knock; if anyone hears My voice and opens the door, I will come in to him and will dine with him, and he with Me.

Revelation 3:20

B-10   Proclaim Christ

Assurance of Salvation   NASB

1 John 5:13

These things I have written to you who believe in the name of the Son of God, so that you may know that you have eternal life.

1 John 5:13

B-11   Proclaim Christ

Assurance of Salvation   NASB

John 5:24

Truly, truly, I say to you, he who hears My word, and believes Him who sent Me, has eternal life, and does not come into judgment, but has passed out of death into life.

John 5:24

B-12   Proclaim Christ

B. Proclaim Christ

B. Proclaim Christ

Must Receive Christ   NKJV
Revelation 3:20

Behold, I stand at the door and knock. If anyone hears My voice and opens the door, I will come in to him and dine with him, and he with Me.

Revelation 3:20

B-10   Proclaim Christ

Must Receive Christ   NKJV
John 1:12

But as many as received Him, to them He gave the right to become children of God, even to those who believe in His name.

John 1:12

B-9   Proclaim Christ

Assurance of Salvation   NKJV
John 5:24

Most assuredly, I say to you, he who hears My word and believes in Him who sent Me has everlasting life, and shall not come into judgment, but has passed from death into life.

John 5:24

B-12   Proclaim Christ

Assurance of Salvation   NKJV
1 John 5:13

These things I have written to you who believe in the name of the Son of God, that you may know that you have eternal life, and that you may continue to believe in the name of the Son of God.

1 John 5:13

B-11   Proclaim Christ

B. Proclaim Christ

B. Proclaim Christ

Must Receive Christ   ESV

John 1:12

But to all who did receive him, who believed in his name, he gave the right to become children of God.

John 1:12

Must Receive Christ   ESV

Revelation 3:20

Behold, I stand at the door and knock. If anyone hears my voice and opens the door, I will come in to him and eat with him, and he with me.

Revelation 3:20

Assurance of Salvation   ESV

1 John 5:13

I write these things to you who believe in the name of the Son of God that you may know that you have eternal life.

1 John 5:13

Assurance of Salvation   ESV

John 5:24

Truly, truly, I say to you, whoever hears my word and believes him who sent me has eternal life. He does not come into judgment, but has passed from death to life.

John 5:24

B. Proclaim Christ

B. Proclaim Christ

Must Receive Christ   KJV

Revelation 3:20

Behold, I stand at the door, and knock: if any man hear my voice, and open the door, I will come in to him, and will sup with him, and he with me.

Revelation 3:20

B-10   Proclaim Christ

Must Receive Christ   KJV

John 1:12

But as many as received him, to them gave he power to become the sons of God, even to them that believe on his name.

John 1:12

B-9   Proclaim Christ

Assurance of Salvation   KJV

John 5:24

Verily, verily, I say unto you, He that heareth my word, and believeth on him that sent me, hath everlasting life, and shall not come into condemnation; but is passed from death unto life.

John 5:24

B-12   Proclaim Christ

Assurance of Salvation   KJV

1 John 5:13

These things have I written unto you that believe on the name of the Son of God; that ye may know that ye have eternal life, and that ye may believe on the name of the Son of God.

1 John 5:13

B-11   Proclaim Christ

Must Receive Christ NRSV

John 1:12

But to all who received him, who believed in his name, he gave power to become children of God.

John 1:12

B-9   Proclaim Christ

Must Receive Christ NRSV

Revelation 3:20

Listen! I am standing at the door, knocking; if you hear my voice and open the door, I will come in to you and eat with you, and you with me.

Revelation 3:20

B-10   Proclaim Christ

Assurance of Salvation NRSV

1 John 5:13

I write these things to you who believe in the name of the Son of God, so that you may know that you have eternal life.

1 John 5:13

B-11   Proclaim Christ

Assurance of Salvation NRSV

John 5:24

Very truly, I tell you, anyone who hears my word and believes him who sent me has eternal life, and does not come under judgment, but has passed from death to life.

John 5:24

B-12   Proclaim Christ

B. Proclaim Christ

B. Proclaim Christ

Must Receive Christ   NLT

Revelation 3:20

Look! Here I stand at the door and knock. If you hear me calling and open the door, I will come in, and we will share a meal as friends.

Revelation 3:20

B-10   Proclaim Christ

Must Receive Christ   NLT

John 1:12

But to all who believed him and accepted him, he gave the right to become children of God.

John 1:12

B-9   Proclaim Christ

Assurance of Salvation   NLT

John 5:24

I assure you, those who listen to my message and believe in God who sent me have eternal life. They will never be condemned for their sins, but they have already passed from death into life.

John 5:24

B-12   Proclaim Christ

Assurance of Salvation   NLT

1 John 5:13

I write this to you who believe in the Son of God, so that you may know you have eternal life.

1 John 5:13

B-11   Proclaim Christ

C. Rely on God's Resources

C. Rely on God's Resources

His Spirit
NIV

1 Corinthians 3:16

Don't you know that you yourselves are God's temple and that God's Spirit dwells in your midst?

1 Corinthians 3:16

His Spirit
NIV

1 Corinthians 2:12

What we have received is not the spirit of the world, but the Spirit who is from God, so that we may understand what God has freely given us.

1 Corinthians 2:12

His Strength
NIV

Isaiah 41:10

So do not fear, for I am with you; do not be dismayed, for I am your God. I will strengthen you and help you; I will uphold you with my righteous right hand.

Isaiah 41:10

His Strength
NIV

Philippians 4:13

I can do all this through him who gives me strength.

Philippians 4:13

His Faithfulness
NIV

Lamentations 3:22-23

Because of the LORD's great love we are not consumed, for his compassions never fail. They are new every morning; great is your faithfulness.

Lamentations 3:22-23

His Faithfulness
NIV

Numbers 23:19

God is not human, that he should lie, not a human being, that he should change his mind. Does he speak and then not act? Does he promise and not fulfill?

Numbers 23:19

His Peace
NIV

Isaiah 26:3

You will keep in perfect peace those whose minds are steadfast, because they trust in you.

Isaiah 26:3

His Peace
NIV

1 Peter 5:7

Cast all your anxiety on him because he cares for you.

1 Peter 5:7

C. Rely on God's Resources

C. Rely on God's Resources

His Spirit   MSG

1 Corinthians 2:12

But he lets *us* in on it. God offers a full report on the gifts of life and salvation that he is giving us.

1 Corinthians 2:12

His Spirit   MSG

1 Corinthians 3:16

You realize, don't you, that you are the temple of God, and God himself is present in you?

1 Corinthians 3:16

His Strength   MSG

Philippians 4:13

Whatever I have, wherever I am, I can make it through anything in the One who makes me who I am.

Philippians 4:13

His Strength   MSG

Isaiah 41:10

Don't panic. I'm with you. There's no need to fear for I'm your God. I'll give you strength. I'll help you. I'll hold you steady, keep a firm grip on you.

Isaiah 41:10

His Faithfulness   MSG

Numbers 23:19

God is not man, one given to lies, and not a son of man changing his mind. Does he speak and not do what he says? Does he promise and not come through?

Numbers 23:19

His Faithfulness   MSG

Lamentations 3:22-23

GOD's loyal love couldn't have run out, his merciful love couldn't have dried up. They're created new every morning. How great your faithfulness!

Lamentations 3:22-23

His Peace   MSG

1 Peter 5:7

Live carefree before God; he is most careful with you.

1 Peter 5:7

His Peace   MSG

Isaiah 26:3

People with their minds set on you, you keep completely whole, steady on their feet, because they keep at it and don't quit.

Isaiah 26:3

C. Rely on God's Resources

C. Rely on God's Resources

His Spirit — NASB
1 Corinthians 3:16

Do you not know that you are a temple of God and that the Spirit of God dwells in you?

1 Corinthians 3:16

C-1 Rely on God's Resources

His Spirit — NASB
1 Corinthians 2:12

Now we have received, not the spirit of the world, but the Spirit who is from God, so that we may know the things freely given to us by God.

1 Corinthians 2:12

C-2 Rely on God's Resources

His Strength — NASB
Isaiah 41:10

Do not fear, for I am with you; do not anxiously look about you, for I am your God. I will strengthen you, surely I will help you, surely I will uphold you with My righteous right hand.

Isaiah 41:10

C-3 Rely on God's Resources

His Strength — NASB
Philippians 4:13

I can do all things through Him who strengthens me.

Philippians 4:13

C-4 Rely on God's Resources

His Faithfulness — NASB
Lamentations 3:22-23

The LORD's lovingkindnesses indeed never cease, for His compassions never fail. They are new every morning; great is Your faithfulness.

Lamentations 3:22-23

C-5 Rely on God's Resources

His Faithfulness — NASB
Numbers 23:19

God is not a man, that He should lie, nor a son of man, that He should repent; has He said, and will He not do it? Or has He spoken, and will He not make it good?

Numbers 23:19

C-6 Rely on God's Resources

His Peace — NASB
Isaiah 26:3

The steadfast of mind You will keep in perfect peace, because he trusts in You.

Isaiah 26:3

C-7 Rely on God's Resources

His Peace — NASB
1 Peter 5:7

Casting all your anxiety on Him, because He cares for you.

1 Peter 5:7

C-8 Rely on God's Resources

C. Rely on God's Resources

C. Rely on God's Resources

His Spirit
NKJV

1 Corinthians 2:12

Now we have received, not the spirit of the world, but the Spirit who is from God, that we might know the things that have been freely given to us by God.

1 Corinthians 2:12

C-2   Rely on God's Resources

His Spirit
NKJV

1 Corinthians 3:16

Do you not know that you are the temple of God and that the Spirit of God dwells in you?

1 Corinthians 3:16

C-1   Rely on God's Resources

His Strength
NKJV

Philippians 4:13

I can do all things through Christ who strengthens me.

Philippians 4:13

C-4   Rely on God's Resources

His Strength
NKJV

Isaiah 41:10

Fear not, for I am with you; be not dismayed, for I am your God. I will strengthen you, yes, I will help you, I will uphold you with My righteous right hand.

Isaiah 41:10

C-3   Rely on God's Resources

His Faithfulness
NKJV

Numbers 23:19

God is not a man, that He should lie, nor a son of man, that He should repent. Has He said, and will He not do it? Or has He spoken, and will He not make it good?

Numbers 23:19

C-6   Rely on God's Resources

His Faithfulness
NKJV

Lamentations 3:22-23

Through the Lord's mercies we are not consumed, because His compassions fail not. They are new every morning; great is Your faithfulness.

Lamentations 3:22-23

C-5   Rely on God's Resources

His Peace
NKJV

1 Peter 5:7

Casting all your care upon Him, for He cares for you.

1 Peter 5:7

C-8   Rely on God's Resources

His Peace
NKJV

Isaiah 26:3

You will keep him in perfect peace, whose mind is stayed on You, because he trusts in You.

Isaiah 26:3

C-7   Rely on God's Resources

C. Rely on God's Resources

C. Rely on God's Resources

His Spirit   ESV

1 Corinthians 3:16

Do you not know that you are God's temple and that God's Spirit dwells in you?

1 Corinthians 3:16

C-1   *Rely on God's Resources*

His Spirit   ESV

1 Corinthians 2:12

Now we have received not the spirit of the world, but the Spirit who is from God, that we might understand the things freely given us by God.

1 Corinthians 2:12

C-2   *Rely on God's Resources*

His Strength   ESV

Isaiah 41:10

Fear not, for I am with you; be not dismayed, for I am your God; I will strengthen you, I will help you, I will uphold you with my righteous right hand.

Isaiah 41:10

C-3   *Rely on God's Resources*

His Strength   ESV

Philippians 4:13

I can do all things through him who strengthens me.

Philippians 4:13

C-4   *Rely on God's Resources*

His Faithfulness   ESV

Lamentations 3:22-23

The steadfast love of the LORD never ceases; his mercies never come to an end; they are new every morning; great is your faithfulness.

Lamentations 3:22-23

C-5   *Rely on God's Resources*

His Faithfulness   ESV

Numbers 23:19

God is not man, that he should lie, or a son of man, that he should change his mind. Has he said, and will he not do it? Or has he spoken, and will he not fulfill it?

Numbers 23:19

C-6   *Rely on God's Resources*

His Peace   ESV

Isaiah 26:3

You keep him in perfect peace whose mind is stayed on you, because he trusts in you.

Isaiah 26:3

C-7   *Rely on God's Resources*

His Peace   ESV

1 Peter 5:7

Casting all your anxieties on him, because he cares for you.

1 Peter 5:7

C-8   *Rely on God's Resources*

C. Rely on God's Resources

C. Rely on God's Resources

His Spirit KJV
1 Corinthians 2:12

Now we have received, not the spirit of the world, but the spirit which is of God; that we might know the things that are freely given to us of God.

1 Corinthians 2:12

His Spirit KJV
1 Corinthians 3:16

Know ye not that ye are the temple of God, and that the Spirit of God dwelleth in you?

1 Corinthians 3:16

His Strength KJV
Philippians 4:13

I can do all things through Christ who strengtheneth me.

Philippians 4:13

His Strength KJV
Isaiah 41:10

Fear thou not; for I am with thee: be not dismayed; for I am thy God: I will strengthen thee; yea, I will help thee; yea, I will uphold thee with the right hand of my righteousness.

Isaiah 41:10

His Faithfulness KJV
Numbers 23:19

God is not a man, that he should lie; neither the son of man, that he should repent: hath he said, and shall he not do it? or hath he spoken, and shall he not make it good?

Numbers 23:19

His Faithfulness KJV
Lamentations 3:22-23

It is of the LORD's mercies that we are not consumed, because his compassions fail not. They are new every morning: great is thy faithfulness.

Lamentations 3:22-23

His Peace KJV
1 Peter 5:7

Casting all your care upon him; for he careth for you.

1 Peter 5:7

His Peace KJV
Isaiah 26:3

Thou wilt keep him in perfect peace, whose mind is stayed on thee: because he trusteth in thee.

Isaiah 26:3

C. Rely on God's Resources

C. Rely on God's Resources

His Spirit
NRSV

1 Corinthians 3:16

Do you not know that you are God's temple and that God's Spirit dwells in you?

1 Corinthians 3:16

C-1   Rely on God's Resources

His Spirit
NRSV

1 Corinthians 2:12

Now we have received not the spirit of the world, but the Spirit that is from God, so that we may understand the gifts bestowed on us by God.

1 Corinthians 2:12

C-2   Rely on God's Resources

His Strength
NRSV

Isaiah 41:10

Do not fear, for I am with you, do not be afraid, for I am your God; I will strengthen you, I will help you, I will uphold you with my victorious right hand.

Isaiah 41:10

C-3   Rely on God's Resources

His Strength
NRSV

Philippians 4:13

I can do all things through him who strengthens me.

Philippians 4:13

C-4   Rely on God's Resources

His Faithfulness
NRSV

Lamentations 3:22-23

The steadfast love of the LORD never ceases, his mercies never come to an end; they are new every morning; great is your faithfulness.

Lamentations 3:22-23

C-5   Rely on God's Resources

His Faithfulness
NRSV

Numbers 23:19

God is not a human being, that he should lie, or a mortal, that he should change his mind. Has he promised, and will he not do it? Has he spoken, and will he not fulfill it?

Numbers 23:19

C-6   Rely on God's Resources

His Peace
NRSV

Isaiah 26:3

Those of steadfast mind you keep in peace — in peace because they trust in you.

Isaiah 26:3

C-7   Rely on God's Resources

His Peace
NRSV

1 Peter 5:7

Cast all your anxiety on him, because he cares for you.

1 Peter 5:7

C-8   Rely on God's Resources

C. Rely on God's Resources

C. Rely on God's Resources

His Spirit   NLT

1 Corinthians 2:12

And God has actually given us his Spirit (not the world's spirit) so we can know the wonderful things God has freely given us.

1 Corinthians 2:12

His Spirit   NLT

1 Corinthians 3:16

Don't you realize that all of you together are the temple of God and that the Spirit of God lives in you?

1 Corinthians 3:16

His Strength   NLT

Philippians 4:13

For I can do everything with the help of Christ who gives me the strength I need.

Philippians 4:13

His Strength   NLT

Isaiah 41:10

Don't be afraid, for I am with you. Do not be dismayed, for I am your God. I will strengthen you. I will help you. I will uphold you with my victorious right hand.

Isaiah 41:10

His Faithfulness   NLT

Numbers 23:19

God is not man, that he should lie. He is not a human, that he should change his mind. Has he ever spoken and failed to act? Has he ever promised and not carried it through?

Numbers 23:19

His Faithfulness   NLT

Lamentations 3:22-23

The unfailing love of the LORD never ends! By his mercies we have been kept from complete destruction. Great is his faithfulness; his mercies begin afresh each day.

Lamentations 3:22-23

His Peace   NLT

1 Peter 5:7

Give all your worries and cares to God, for he cares about what happens to you.

1 Peter 5:7

His Peace   NLT

Isaiah 26:3

You will keep in perfect peace all who trust in you, whose thoughts are fixed on you!

Isaiah 26:3

C. Rely on God's Resources

C. Rely on God's Resources

His Provision   NIV
Romans 8:32

He who did not spare his own Son, but gave him up for us all — how will he not also, along with him, graciously give us all things?

Romans 8:32

C-9   Rely on God's Resources

His Provision   NIV
Philippians 4:19

And my God will meet all your needs according to the riches of his glory in Christ Jesus.

Philippians 4:19

C-10   Rely on God's Resources

His Help in Temptation   NIV
Hebrews 2:18

Because he himself suffered when he was tempted, he is able to help those who are being tempted.

Hebrews 2:18

C-11   Rely on God's Resources

His Help in Temptation   NIV
Psalm 119:9,11

How can a young person stay on the path of purity? By living according to your word. . . . I have hidden your word in my heart that I might not sin against you.

Psalm 119:9, 11

C-12   Rely on God's Resources

TOPICAL MEMORY SYSTEM
A. Live the New Life
Christ the Center—2 Corinthians 5:17; Galatians 2:20
Obedience to Christ—Romans 12:1; John 14:21
God's Word—2 Timothy 3:16; Joshua 1:8
Prayer—John 15:7; Philippians 4:6-7
Fellowship—1 John 1:3; Hebrews 10:24-25
Witnessing—Matthew 4:19; Romans 1:16
B. Proclaim Christ
All Have Sinned—Romans 3:23; Isaiah 53:6
Sin's Penalty—Romans 6:23; Hebrews 9:27
Christ Paid the Penalty—Romans 5:8; 1 Peter 3:18
Salvation Not by Works—Ephesians 2:8-9; Titus 3:5
Must Receive Christ—John 1:12; Revelation 3:20
Assurance of Salvation—1 John 5:13; John 5:24

C. Rely on God's Resources
His Spirit—1 Corinthians 3:16; 1 Corinthians 2:12
His Strength—Isaiah 41:10; Philippians 4:13
His Faithfulness—Lamentations 3:22-23; Numbers 23:19
His Peace—Isaiah 26:3; 1 Peter 5:7
His Provision—Romans 8:32; Philippians 4:19
His Help in Temptation—Hebrews 2:18; Psalm 119:9, 11
D. Be Christ's Disciple
Put Christ First—Matthew 6:33; Luke 9:23
Separate from the World—1 John 2:15-16; Romans 12:2
Be Steadfast—1 Corinthians 15:58; Hebrews 12:3
Serve Others—Mark 10:45; 2 Corinthians 4:5
Give Generously—Proverbs 3:9-10; 2 Corinthians 9:6-7
Develop World Vision—Acts 1:8; Matthew 28:19-20

TOPICAL MEMORY SYSTEM (cont)
E. Grow in Christlikeness
Love—John 13:34-35; 1 John 3:18
Humility—Philippians 2:3-4; 1 Peter 5:5-6
Purity—Ephesians 5:3; 1 Peter 2:11
Honesty—Leviticus 19:11; Acts 24:16
Faith—Hebrews 11:6; Romans 4:20-21
Good Works—Galatians 6:9-10; Matthew 5:16

© The Navigators 1969, 1981, 2006

This Pack Belongs To

Name _____

Address _____

_____

Phone _____

If found, please return to above address.

C. Rely on God's Resources

C. Rely on God's Resources

His Provision   MSG

Philippians 4:19

You can be sure that God will take care of everything you need, his generosity exceeding even yours in the glory that pours from Jesus.

Philippians 4:19

C-10   *Rely on God's Resources*

His Provision   MSG

Romans 8:32

If God didn't hesitate to put everything on the line for us, embracing our condition and exposing himself to the worst by sending his own Son, is there anything else he wouldn't gladly and freely do for us?

Romans 8:32

C-9   *Rely on God's Resources*

His Help in Temptation   MSG

Psalm 119:9,11

How can a young person live a clean life? By carefully reading the map of your Word. . . . I've banked your promises in the vault of my heart so I won't sin myself bankrupt.

Psalm 119:9, 11

C-12   *Rely on God's Resources*

His Help in Temptation   MSG

Hebrews 2:18

He would have already experienced it all himself — all the pain, all the testing — and would be able to help where help was needed.

Hebrews 2:18

C-11   *Rely on God's Resources*

C. Rely on God's Resources

C. Rely on God's Resources

His Provision   NASB

Romans 8:32

He who did not spare His own Son, but delivered Him over for us all, how will He not also with Him freely give us all things?

Romans 8:32

C-9   *Rely on God's Resources*

His Provision   NASB

Philippians 4:19

And my God will supply all your needs according to His riches in glory in Christ Jesus.

Philippians 4:19

C-10   *Rely on God's Resources*

His Help in Temptation   NASB

Hebrews 2:18

For since He Himself was tempted in that which He has suffered, He is able to come to the aid of those who are tempted.

Hebrews 2:18

C-11   *Rely on God's Resources*

His Help in Temptation   NASB

Psalm 119:9,11

How can a young man keep his way pure? By keeping it according to Your word. . . . Your word I have treasured in my heart, that I may not sin against You.

Psalm 119:9, 11

C-12   *Rely on God's Resources*

C. Rely on God's Resources

C. Rely on God's Resources

His Provision   NKJV

Philippians 4:19

    And my God shall supply all your need according to His riches in glory by Christ Jesus.

Philippians 4:19

C-10   *Rely on God's Resources*

His Provision   NKJV

Romans 8:32

    He who did not spare His own Son, but delivered Him up for us all, how shall He not with Him also freely give us all things?

Romans 8:32

C-9   *Rely on God's Resources*

His Help in Temptation   NKJV

Psalm 119:9,11

    How can a young man cleanse his way? By taking heed according to Your word. . . . Your word I have hidden in my heart, that I might not sin against You.

Psalm 119:9, 11

C-12   *Rely on God's Resources*

His Help in Temptation   NKJV

Hebrews 2:18

    For in that He Himself has suffered, being tempted, He is able to aid those who are tempted.

Hebrews 2:18

C-11   *Rely on God's Resources*

C. Rely on God's Resources

C. Rely on God's Resources

His Provision
ESV

Romans 8:32

He who did not spare his own Son but gave him up for us all, how will he not also with him graciously give us all things?

Romans 8:32

C-9   Rely on God's Resources

His Provision
ESV

Philippians 4:19

And my God will supply every need of yours according to his riches in glory in Christ Jesus.

Philippians 4:19

C-10   Rely on God's Resources

His Help in Temptation
ESV

Hebrews 2:18

For because he himself has suffered when tempted, he is able to help those who are being tempted.

Hebrews 2:18

C-11   Rely on God's Resources

His Help in Temptation
ESV

Psalm 119:9,11

How can a young man keep his way pure? By guarding it according to your word. . . . I have stored up your word in my heart, that I might not sin against you.

Psalm 119:9, 11

C-12   Rely on God's Resources

C. Rely on God's Resources

C. Rely on God's Resources

His Provision   KJV

Philippians 4:19

But my God shall supply all your need according to his riches in glory by Christ Jesus.

Philippians 4:19

C-10   Rely on God's Resources

His Provision   KJV

Romans 8:32

He that spared not his own Son, but delivered him up for us all, how shall he not with him also freely give us all things?

Romans 8:32

C-9   Rely on God's Resources

His Help in Temptation   KJV

Psalm 119:9,11

Wherewithal shall a young man cleanse his way? by taking heed thereto according to thy word. . . . Thy word have I hid in mine heart, that I might not sin against thee.

Psalm 119:9, 11

C-12   Rely on God's Resources

His Help in Temptation   KJV

Hebrews 2:18

For in that he himself hath suffered being tempted, he is able to succour them that are tempted.

Hebrews 2:18

C-11   Rely on God's Resources

C. Rely on God's Resources

C. Rely on God's Resources

His Provision — NRSV
Romans 8:32

He who did not withhold his own Son, but gave him up for all of us, will he not with him also give us everything else?

Romans 8:32

C-9   Rely on God's Resources

His Provision — NRSV
Philippians 4:19

And my God will fully satisfy every need of yours according to his riches in glory in Christ Jesus.

Philippians 4:19

C-10   Rely on God's Resources

His Help in Temptation — NRSV
Hebrews 2:18

Because he himself was tested by what he suffered, he is able to help those who are being tested.

Hebrews 2:18

C-11   Rely on God's Resources

His Help in Temptation — NRSV
Psalm 119:9,11

How can young people keep their way pure? By guarding it according to your word. . . . I treasure your word in my heart, so that I may not sin against you.

Psalm 119:9, 11

C-12   Rely on God's Resources

C. Rely on God's Resources

C. Rely on God's Resources

His Provision   NLT

Philippians 4:19

And this same God who takes care of me will supply all your needs from his glorious riches, which have been given to us in Christ Jesus.

Philippians 4:19

C-10   Rely on God's Resources

His Provision   NLT

Romans 8:32

Since God did not spare even his own Son but gave him up for us all, won't God, who gave us Christ, also give us everything else?

Romans 8:32

C-9   Rely on God's Resources

His Help in Temptation   NLT

Psalm 119:9,11

How can a young person stay pure? By obeying your word and following its rules. . . . I have hidden your word in my heart, that I might not sin against you.

Psalm 119:9, 11

C-12   Rely on God's Resources

His Help in Temptation   NLT

Hebrews 2:18

Since he himself has gone through suffering and temptation, he is able to help us when we are being tempted.

Hebrews 2:18

C-11   Rely on God's Resources

D. Be Christ's Disciple

D. Be Christ's Disciple

Put Christ First
NIV

Matthew 6:33

But seek first his kingdom and his righteousness, and all these things will be given to you as well.

Matthew 6:33

D-1   Be Christ's Disciple

Put Christ First
NIV

Luke 9:23

Then he said to them all: "Whoever wants to be my disciple must deny themselves and take up their cross daily and follow me."

Luke 9:23

D-2   Be Christ's Disciple

Separate from the World
NIV

1 John 2:15-16

Do not love the world or anything in the world. If anyone loves the world, love for the Father is not in them. For everything in the world — the lust of the flesh, the lust of the eyes, and the pride of life — comes not from the Father but from the world.

1 John 2:15-16

D-3   Be Christ's Disciple

Separate from the World
NIV

Romans 12:2

Do not conform to the pattern of this world, but be transformed by the renewing of your mind. Then you will be able to test and approve what God's will is — his good, pleasing and perfect will.

Romans 12:2

D-4   Be Christ's Disciple

Be Steadfast
NIV

1 Corinthians 15:58

Therefore, my dear brothers and sisters, stand firm. Let nothing move you. Always give yourselves fully to the work of the Lord, because you know that your labor in the Lord is not in vain.

1 Corinthians 15:58

D-5   Be Christ's Disciple

Be Steadfast
NIV

Hebrews 12:3

Consider him who endured such opposition from sinners, so that you will not grow weary and lose heart.

Hebrews 12:3

D-6   Be Christ's Disciple

Serve Others
NIV

Mark 10:45

For even the Son of Man did not come to be served, but to serve, and to give his life as a ransom for many.

Mark 10:45

D-7   Be Christ's Disciple

Serve Others
NIV

2 Corinthians 4:5

For what we preach is not ourselves, but Jesus Christ as Lord, and ourselves as your servants for Jesus' sake.

2 Corinthians 4:5

D-8   Be Christ's Disciple

D. Be Christ's Disciple

D. Be Christ's Disciple

Put Christ First   MSG
Luke 9:23

Then he told them what they could expect for themselves: "Anyone who intends to come with me has to let me lead. You're not in the driver's seat — I am. Don't run from suffering; embrace it. Follow me and I'll show you how."

Luke 9:23

D-2   Be Christ's Disciple

Put Christ First   MSG
Matthew 6:33

Steep your life in God-reality, God-initiative, God-provisions. Don't worry about missing out. You'll find all your everyday human concerns will be met.

Matthew 6:33

D-1   Be Christ's Disciple

Separate from the World   MSG
Romans 12:2

Don't become so well-adjusted to your culture that you fit into it without even thinking. Instead, fix your attention on God. You'll be changed from the inside out. Readily recognize what he wants from you, and quickly respond to it. Unlike the culture around you, always dragging you down to its level of immaturity, God brings the best out of you, develops well-formed maturity in you.

Romans 12:2

D-4   Be Christ's Disciple

Separate from the World   MSG
1 John 2:15-16

Don't love the world's ways. Don't love the world's goods. Love of the world squeezes out love for the Father. Practically everything that goes on in the world — wanting your own way, wanting everything for yourself, wanting to appear important — has nothing to do with the Father. It just isolates you from him.

1 John 2:15-16

D-6   Be Christ's Disciple

D-3   Be Christ's Disciple

Be Steadfast   MSG
Hebrews 12:3

When you find yourselves flagging in your faith, go over that story again, item by item, that long litany of hostility he plowed through. *That* will shoot adrenaline into your souls!

Hebrews 12:3

Be Steadfast   MSG
1 Corinthians 15:58

With all this going for us, my dear, dear friends, stand your ground. And don't hold back. Throw yourselves into the work of the Master, confident that nothing you do for him is a waste of time or effort.

1 Corinthians 15:58

D-5   Be Christ's Disciple

Serve Others   MSG
2 Corinthians 4:5

Remember, our Message is not about ourselves; we're proclaiming Jesus Christ, the Master. All we are is messengers, errand runners from Jesus for you.

2 Corinthians 4:5

D-8   Be Christ's Disciple

Serve Others   MSG
Mark 10:45

That is what the Son of Man has done: He came to serve, not to be served — and then to give away his life in exchange for many who are held hostage.

Mark 10:45

D. Be Christ's Disciple

D. Be Christ's Disciple

Put Christ First   NASB

Matthew 6:33

But seek first His kingdom and His righteousness, and all these things will be added to you.

Matthew 6:33

Put Christ First   NASB

Luke 9:23

And He was saying to them all, "If anyone wishes to come after Me, he must deny himself, and take up his cross daily and follow Me."

Luke 9:23

Separate from the World   NASB

1 John 2:15-16

Do not love the world nor the things in the world. If anyone loves the world, the love of the Father is not in him. For all that is in the world, the lust of the flesh and the lust of the eyes and the boastful pride of life, is not from the Father, but is from the world.

1 John 2:15-16

Separate from the World   NASB

Romans 12:2

And do not be conformed to this world, but be transformed by the renewing of your mind, so that you may prove what the will of God is, that which is good and acceptable and perfect.

Romans 12:2

Be Steadfast   NASB

1 Corinthians 15:58

Therefore, my beloved brethren, be steadfast, immovable, always abounding in the work of the Lord, knowing that your toil is not in vain in the Lord.

1 Corinthians 15:58

Be Steadfast   NASB

Hebrews 12:3

For consider Him who has endured such hostility by sinners against Himself, so that you will not grow weary and lose heart.

Hebrews 12:3

Serve Others   NASB

Mark 10:45

For even the Son of Man did not come to be served, but to serve, and to give His life a ransom for many.

Mark 10:45

Serve Others   NASB

2 Corinthians 4:5

For we do not preach ourselves but Christ Jesus as Lord, and ourselves as your bond-servants for Jesus' sake.

2 Corinthians 4:5

Put Christ First
NKJV

Luke 9:23

Then He said to them all, "If anyone desires to come after Me, let him deny himself, and take up his cross daily, and follow Me."

Luke 9:23

D-2   Be Christ's Disciple

Put Christ First
NKJV

Matthew 6:33

But seek first the kingdom of God and His righteousness, and all these things shall be added to you.

Matthew 6:33

D-1   Be Christ's Disciple

Separate from the World
NKJV

Romans 12:2

And do not be conformed to this world, but be transformed by the renewing of your mind, that you may prove what is that good and acceptable and perfect will of God.

Romans 12:2

D-4   Be Christ's Disciple

Separate from the World
NKJV

1 John 2:15-16

Do not love the world or the things in the world. If anyone loves the world, the love of the Father is not in him. For all that is in the world — the lust of the flesh, the lust of the eyes, and the pride of life — is not of the Father but is of the world.

1 John 2:15-16

D-3   Be Christ's Disciple

Be Steadfast
NKJV

Hebrews 12:3

For consider Him who endured such hostility from sinners against Himself, lest you become weary and discouraged in your souls.

Hebrews 12:3

D-6   Be Christ's Disciple

Be Steadfast
NKJV

1 Corinthians 15:58

Therefore, my beloved brethren, be steadfast, immovable, always abounding in the work of the Lord, knowing that your labor is not in vain in the Lord.

1 Corinthians 15:58

D-5   Be Christ's Disciple

Serve Others
NKJV

2 Corinthians 4:5

For we do not preach ourselves, but Christ Jesus the Lord, and ourselves your servants for Jesus' sake.

2 Corinthians 4:5

D-8   Be Christ's Disciple

Serve Others
NKJV

Mark 10:45

For even the Son of Man did not come to be served, but to serve, and to give His life a ransom for many.

Mark 10:45

D-7   Be Christ's Disciple

D. Be Christ's Disciple

D. Be Christ's Disciple

Put Christ First
ESV

Matthew 6:33

But seek first the kingdom of God and his righteousness, and all these things will be added to you.

Matthew 6:33

D-1   Be Christ's Disciple

Put Christ First
ESV

Luke 9:23

And he said to all, "If anyone would come after me, let him deny himself and take up his cross daily and follow me."

Luke 9:23

D-2   Be Christ's Disciple

Separate from the World
ESV

1 John 2:15-16

Do not love the world or the things in the world. If anyone loves the world, the love of the Father is not in him. For all that is in the world — the desires of the flesh and the desires of the eyes and pride in possessions — is not from the Father but is from the world.

1 John 2:15-16

D-3   Be Christ's Disciple

Separate from the World
ESV

Romans 12:2

Do not be conformed to this world, but be transformed by the renewal of your mind, that by testing you may discern what is the will of God, what is good and acceptable and perfect.

Romans 12:2

D-4   Be Christ's Disciple

Be Steadfast
ESV

1 Corinthians 15:58

Therefore, my beloved brothers, be steadfast, immovable, always abounding in the work of the Lord, knowing that in the Lord your labor is not in vain.

1 Corinthians 15:58

D-5   Be Christ's Disciple

Be Steadfast
ESV

Hebrews 12:3

Consider him who endured from sinners such hostility against himself, so that you may not grow weary or fainthearted.

Hebrews 12:3

D-6   Be Christ's Disciple

Serve Others
ESV

Mark 10:45

For even the Son of Man came not to be served but to serve, and to give his life as a ransom for many.

Mark 10:45

D-7   Be Christ's Disciple

Serve Others
ESV

2 Corinthians 4:5

For what we proclaim is not ourselves, but Jesus Christ as Lord, with ourselves as your servants for Jesus' sake.

2 Corinthians 4:5

D-8   Be Christ's Disciple

D. Be Christ's Disciple

D. Be Christ's Disciple

Put Christ First   KJV

Luke 9:23

And he said to them all, If any man will come after me, let him deny himself, and take up his cross daily, and follow me.

Luke 9:23

D-2   Be Christ's Disciple

Put Christ First   KJV

Matthew 6:33

But seek ye first the kingdom of God, and his righteousness; and all these things shall be added unto you.

Matthew 6:33

D-1   Be Christ's Disciple

Separate from the World   KJV

Romans 12:2

And be not conformed to this world: but be ye transformed by the renewing of your mind, that ye may prove what is that good, and acceptable, and perfect, will of God.

Romans 12:2

D-4   Be Christ's Disciple

Separate from the World   KJV

1 John 2:15-16

Love not the world, neither the things that are in the world. If any man love the world, the love of the Father is not in him. For all that is in the world, the lust of the flesh, and the lust of the eyes, and the pride of life, is not of the Father, but is of the world.

1 John 2:15-16

D-3   Be Christ's Disciple

Be Steadfast   KJV

Hebrews 12:3

For consider him that endured such contradiction of sinners against himself, lest ye be wearied and faint in your minds.

Hebrews 12:3

D-6   Be Christ's Disciple

Be Steadfast   KJV

1 Corinthians 15:58

Therefore, my beloved brethren, be ye steadfast, unmoveable, always abounding in the work of the Lord, forasmuch as ye know that your labour is not in vain in the Lord.

1 Corinthians 15:58

D-5   Be Christ's Disciple

Serve Others   KJV

2 Corinthians 4:5

For we preach not ourselves, but Christ Jesus the Lord; and ourselves your servants for Jesus' sake.

2 Corinthians 4:5

D-8   Be Christ's Disciple

Serve Others   KJV

Mark 10:45

For even the Son of man came not to be ministered unto, but to minister, and to give his life a ransom for many.

Mark 10:45

D-7   Be Christ's Disciple

D. Be Christ's Disciple

D. Be Christ's Disciple

Put Christ First   NRSV

Matthew 6:33

But strive first for the kingdom of God and his righteousness, and all these things will be given to you as well.

Matthew 6:33

Put Christ First   NRSV

Luke 9:23

Then he said to them all, "If any want to become my followers, let them deny themselves and take up their cross daily and follow me."

Luke 9:23

Separate from the World   NRSV

1 John 2:15-16

Do not love the world or the things in the world. The love of the Father is not in those who love the world; for all that is in the world — the desire of the flesh, the desire of the eyes, the pride in riches — comes not from the Father but from the world.

1 John 2:15-16

Separate from the World   NRSV

Romans 12:2

Do not be conformed to this world, but be transformed by the renewing of your minds, so that you may discern what is the will of God — what is good and acceptable and perfect.

Romans 12:2

Be Steadfast   NRSV

1 Corinthians 15:58

Therefore, my beloved, be steadfast, immovable, always excelling in the work of the Lord, because you know that in the Lord your labor is not in vain.

1 Corinthians 15:58

Be Steadfast   NRSV

Hebrews 12:3

Consider him who endured such hostility against himself from sinners, so that you may not grow weary or lose heart.

Hebrews 12:3

Serve Others   NRSV

Mark 10:45

For the Son of Man came not to be served but to serve, and to give his life a ransom for many.

Mark 10:45

Serve Others   NRSV

2 Corinthians 4:5

For we do not proclaim ourselves; we proclaim Jesus Christ as Lord and ourselves as your slaves for Jesus' sake.

2 Corinthians 4:5

D. Be Christ's Disciple

D. Be Christ's Disciple

Put Christ First NLT

Luke 9:23

Then he said to the crowd, "If any of you wants to be my follower, you must put aside your selfish ambition, shoulder your cross daily, and follow me."

Luke 9:23

D-2   Be Christ's Disciple

Put Christ First NLT

Matthew 6:33

And he will give you all you need from day to day if you live for him and make the Kingdom of God your primary concern.

Matthew 6:33

D-1   Be Christ's Disciple

Separate from the World NLT

Romans 12:2

Don't copy the behavior and customs of this world, but let God transform you into a new person by changing the way you think. Then you will know what God wants you to do, and you will know how good and pleasing and perfect his will really is.

Romans 12:2

D-4   Be Christ's Disciple

Separate from the World NLT

1 John 2:15-16

Stop loving this evil world and all that it offers you, for when you love the world, you show that you do not have the love of the Father in you. For the world offers only the lust for physical pleasure, the lust for everything we see, and pride in our possessions. These are not from the Father. They are from this evil world.

1 John 2:15-16

D-3   Be Christ's Disciple

Be Steadfast NLT

Hebrews 12:3

Think about all he endured when sinful people did such terrible things to him, so that you don't become weary and give up.

Hebrews 12:3

D-6   Be Christ's Disciple

Be Steadfast NLT

1 Corinthians 15:58

So, my dear brothers and sisters, be strong and steady, always enthusiastic about the Lord's work, for you know that nothing you do for the Lord is ever useless.

1 Corinthians 15:58

D-5   Be Christ's Disciple

Serve Others NLT

2 Corinthians 4:5

We don't go around preaching about ourselves; we preach Christ Jesus, the Lord. All we say about ourselves is that we are your servants because of what Jesus has done for us.

2 Corinthians 4:5

D-8   Be Christ's Disciple

Serve Others NLT

Mark 10:45

For even I, the Son of Man, came here not to be served but to serve others, and to give my life as a ransom for many.

Mark 10:45

D-7   Be Christ's Disciple

D. Be Christ's Disciple

D. Be Christ's Disciple

Give Generously   NIV

Proverbs 3:9-10

Honor the LORD with your wealth, with the firstfruits of all your crops; then your barns will be filled to overflowing, and your vats will brim over with new wine.

Proverbs 3:9-10

D-9   Be Christ's Disciple

Give Generously   NIV

2 Corinthians 9:6-7

Remember this: Whoever sows sparingly will also reap sparingly, and whoever sows generously will also reap generously. Each of you should give what you have decided in your heart to give, not reluctantly or under compulsion, for God loves a cheerful giver.

2 Corinthians 9:6-7

D-10   Be Christ's Disciple

Develop World Vision   NIV

Acts 1:8

But you will receive power when the Holy Spirit comes on you; and you will be my witnesses in Jerusalem, and in all Judea and Samaria, and to the ends of the earth.

Acts 1:8

D-11   Be Christ's Disciple

Develop World Vision   NIV

Matthew 28:19-20

Therefore go and make disciples of all nations, baptizing them in the name of the Father and of the Son and of the Holy Spirit, and teaching them to obey everything I have commanded you. And surely I am with you always, to the very end of the age.

Matthew 28:19-20

D-12   Be Christ's Disciple

TOPICAL MEMORY SYSTEM

A. Live the New Life
Christ the Center—2 Corinthians 5:17; Galatians 2:20
Obedience to Christ—Romans 12:1; John 14:21
God's Word—2 Timothy 3:16; Joshua 1:8
Prayer—John 15:7; Philippians 4:6-7
Fellowship—1 John 1:3; Hebrews 10:24-25
Witnessing—Matthew 4:19; Romans 1:16

B. Proclaim Christ
All Have Sinned—Romans 3:23; Isaiah 53:6
Sin's Penalty—Romans 6:23; Hebrews 9:27
Christ Paid the Penalty—Romans 5:8; 1 Peter 3:18
Salvation Not by Works—Ephesians 2:8-9; Titus 3:5
Must Receive Christ—John 1:12; Revelation 3:20
Assurance of Salvation—1 John 5:13; John 5:24

C. Rely on God's Resources
His Spirit—1 Corinthians 3:16; 1 Corinthians 2:12
His Strength—Isaiah 41:10; Philippians 4:13
His Faithfulness—Lamentations 3:22-23; Numbers 23:19
His Peace—Isaiah 26:3; 1 Peter 5:7
His Provision—Romans 8:32; Philippians 4:19
His Help in Temptation—Hebrews 2:18; Psalm 119:9, 11

D. Be Christ's Disciple
Put Christ First—Matthew 6:33; Luke 9:23
Separate from the World—1 John 2:15-16; Romans 12:2
Be Steadfast—1 Corinthians 15:58; Hebrews 12:3
Serve Others—Mark 10:45; 2 Corinthians 4:5
Give Generously—Proverbs 3:9-10; 2 Corinthians 9:6-7
Develop World Vision—Acts 1:8; Matthew 28:19-20

TOPICAL MEMORY SYSTEM (cont)

E. Grow in Christlikeness
Love—John 13:34-35; 1 John 3:18
Humility—Philippians 2:3-4; 1 Peter 5:5-6
Purity—Ephesians 5:3; 1 Peter 2:11
Honesty—Leviticus 19:11; Acts 24:16
Faith—Hebrews 11:6; Romans 4:20-21
Good Works—Galatians 6:9-10; Matthew 5:16

© The Navigators 1969, 1981, 2006

This Pack Belongs To

Name _____

Address _____

_____

Phone _____

If found, please return to above address.

D. Be Christ's Disciple

D. Be Christ's Disciple

Give Generously MSG

2 Corinthians 9:6-7

Remember: A stingy planter gets a stingy crop; a lavish planter gets a lavish crop. I want each of you to take plenty of time to think it over, and make up your own mind what you will give. That will protect you against sob stories and arm-twisting. God loves it when the giver delights in the giving.

2 Corinthians 9:6-7

D-10   Be Christ's Disciple

Give Generously MSG

Proverbs 3:9-10

Honor GOD with everything you own; give him the first and the best. Your barns will burst, your wine vats will brim over.

Proverbs 3:9-10

D-9   Be Christ's Disciple

Develop World Vision MSG

Matthew 28:19-20

Go out and train everyone you meet, far and near, in this way of life, marking them by baptism in the threefold name: Father, Son, and Holy Spirit. Then instruct them in the practice of all I have commanded you. I'll be with you as you do this, day after day after day, right up to the end of the age.

Matthew 28:19-20

D-12   Be Christ's Disciple

Develop World Vision MSG

Acts 1:8

What you'll get is the Holy Spirit. And when the Holy Spirit comes on you, you will be able to be my witnesses in Jerusalem, all over Judea and Samaria, even to the ends of the world.

Acts 1:8

D-11   Be Christ's Disciple

D. Be Christ's Disciple

D. Be Christ's Disciple

Give Generously
NASB

Proverbs 3:9-10

Honor the LORD from your wealth and from the first of all your produce; so your barns will be filled with plenty and your vats will overflow with new wine.

Proverbs 3:9-10

D-9   Be Christ's Disciple

Give Generously
NASB

2 Corinthians 9:6-7

Now this I say, he who sows sparingly will also reap sparingly, and he who sows bountifully will also reap bountifully. Each one must do just as he has purposed in his heart, not grudgingly or under compulsion, for God loves a cheerful giver.

2 Corinthians 9:6-7

D-10   Be Christ's Disciple

Develop World Vision
NASB

Acts 1:8

But you will receive power when the Holy Spirit has come upon you; and you shall be My witnesses both in Jerusalem, and in all Judea and Samaria, and even to the remotest part of the earth.

Acts 1:8

D-11   Be Christ's Disciple

Develop World Vision
NASB

Matthew 28:19-20

Go therefore and make disciples of all the nations, baptizing them in the name of the Father and the Son and the Holy Spirit, teaching them to observe all that I commanded you; and lo, I am with you always, even to the end of the age.

Matthew 28:19-20

D-12   Be Christ's Disciple

D. Be Christ's Disciple

D. Be Christ's Disciple

Give Generously NKJV

2 Corinthians 9:6-7

But this I say: He who sows sparingly will also reap sparingly, and he who sows bountifully will also reap bountifully. So let each one give as he purposes in his heart, not grudgingly or of necessity; for God loves a cheerful giver.

2 Corinthians 9:6-7

D-10   Be Christ's Disciple

Give Generously NKJV

Proverbs 3:9-10

Honor the LORD with your possessions, and with the firstfruits of all your increase; so your barns will be filled with plenty, and your vats will overflow with new wine.

Proverbs 3:9-10

D-9   Be Christ's Disciple

Develop World Vision NKJV

Matthew 28:19-20

Go therefore and make disciples of all the nations, baptizing them in the name of the Father and of the Son and of the Holy Spirit, teaching them to observe all things that I have commanded you; and lo, I am with you always, even to the end of the age.

Matthew 28:19-20

D-12   Be Christ's Disciple

Develop World Vision NKJV

Acts 1:8

But you shall receive power when the Holy Spirit has come upon you; and you shall be witnesses to Me in Jerusalem, and in all Judea and Samaria, and to the end of the earth.

Acts 1:8

D-11   Be Christ's Disciple

D. Be Christ's Disciple

D. Be Christ's Disciple

Give Generously   ESV

Proverbs 3:9-10

Honor the Lord with your wealth and with the firstfruits of all your produce; then your barns will be filled with plenty, and your vats will be bursting with wine.

Proverbs 3:9-10

D-9   Be Christ's Disciple

Give Generously   ESV

2 Corinthians 9:6-7

The point is this: whoever sows sparingly will also reap sparingly, and whoever sows bountifully will also reap bountifully. Each one must give as he has made up his mind, not reluctantly or under compulsion, for God loves a cheerful giver.

2 Corinthians 9:6-7

D-10   Be Christ's Disciple

Develop World Vision   ESV

Acts 1:8

But you will receive power when the Holy Spirit has come upon you, and you will be my witnesses in Jerusalem and in all Judea and Samaria, and to the end of the earth.

Acts 1:8

D-11   Be Christ's Disciple

Develop World Vision   ESV

Matthew 28:19-20

Go therefore and make disciples of all nations, baptizing them in the name of the Father and of the Son and of the Holy Spirit, teaching them to observe all that I have commanded you. And behold, I am with you always, to the end of the age.

Matthew 28:19-20

D-12   Be Christ's Disciple

D. Be Christ's Disciple

D. Be Christ's Disciple

Give Generously KJV

2 Corinthians 9:6-7

But this I say, He which soweth sparingly shall reap also sparingly; and he which soweth bountifully shall reap also bountifully. Every man according as he purposeth in his heart, so let him give; not grudgingly, or of necessity: for God loveth a cheerful giver.

2 Corinthians 9:6-7

D-10   Be Christ's Disciple

Give Generously KJV

Proverbs 3:9-10

Honour the LORD with thy substance, and with the firstfruits of all thine increase: So shall thy barns be filled with plenty, and thy presses shall burst out with new wine.

Proverbs 3:9-10

D-9   Be Christ's Disciple

Develop World Vision KJV

Matthew 28:19-20

Go ye therefore, and teach all nations, baptizing them in the name of the Father, and of the Son, and of the Holy Ghost: Teaching them to observe all things whatsoever I have commanded you: and, lo, I am with you always, even unto the end of the world. Amen.

Matthew 28:19-20

D-12   Be Christ's Disciple

Develop World Vision KJV

Acts 1:8

But ye shall receive power, after that the Holy Ghost is come upon you: and ye shall be witnesses unto me both in Jerusalem, and in all Judaea, and in Samaria, and unto the uttermost part of the earth.

Acts 1:8

D-11   Be Christ's Disciple

D. Be Christ's Disciple

D. Be Christ's Disciple

Give Generously   NRSV

Proverbs 3:9-10

Honor the LORD with your substance and with the first fruits of all your produce; then your barns will be filled with plenty, and your vats will be bursting with wine.

Proverbs 3:9-10

D-9   Be Christ's Disciple

Give Generously   NRSV

2 Corinthians 9:6-7

The point is this: the one who sows sparingly will also reap sparingly, and the one who sows bountifully will also reap bountifully. Each of you must give as you have made up your mind, not reluctantly or under compulsion, for God loves a cheerful giver.

2 Corinthians 9:6-7

D-10   Be Christ's Disciple

Develop World Vision   NRSV

Acts 1:8

But you will receive power when the Holy Spirit has come upon you; and you will be my witnesses in Jerusalem, in all Judea and Samaria, and to the ends of the earth.

Acts 1:8

D-11   Be Christ's Disciple

Develop World Vision   NRSV

Matthew 28:19-20

Go therefore and make disciples of all nations, baptizing them in the name of the Father and of the Son and of the Holy Spirit, and teaching them to obey everything that I have commanded you. And remember, I am with you always, to the end of the age.

Matthew 28:19-20

D-12   Be Christ's Disciple

D. Be Christ's Disciple

D. Be Christ's Disciple

Give Generously   NLT

2 Corinthians 9:6-7

Remember this—a farmer who plants only a few seeds will get a small crop. But the one who plants generously will get a generous crop. You must each make up your own mind as to how much you should give. Don't give reluctantly or in response to pressure. For God loves the person who gives cheerfully.

2 Corinthians 9:6-7

D-10   Be Christ's Disciple

Give Generously   NLT

Proverbs 3:9-10

Honor the Lord with your wealth and with the best part of everything your land produces. Then he will fill your barns with grain, and your vats will overflow with the finest wine.

Proverbs 3:9-10

D-9   Be Christ's Disciple

Develop World Vision   NLT

Matthew 28:19-20

Therefore, go and make disciples of all the nations, baptizing them in the name of the Father and the Son and the Holy Spirit. Teach these new disciples to obey all the commands I have given you. And be sure of this: I am with you always, even to the end of the age.

Matthew 28:19-20

D-12   Be Christ's Disciple

Develop World Vision   NLT

Acts 1:8

But when the Holy Spirit has come upon you, you will receive power and will tell people about me everywhere — in Jerusalem, throughout Judea, in Samaria, and to the ends of the earth.

Acts 1:8

D-11   Be Christ's Disciple

E. Grow in Christlikeness

E. Grow in Christlikeness

Love   NIV
John 13:34-35

A new command I give you: Love one another. As I have loved you, so you must love one another. By this everyone will know that you are my disciples, if you love one another.

John 13:34-35

E-1   *Grow in Christlikeness*

Love   NIV
1 John 3:18

Dear children, let us not love with words or speech but with actions and in truth.

1 John 3:18

E-2   *Grow in Christlikeness*

Humility   NIV
Philippians 2:3-4

Do nothing out of selfish ambition or vain conceit. Rather, in humility value others above yourselves, not looking to your own interests but each of you to the interests of the others.

Philippians 2:3-4

E-3   *Grow in Christlikeness*

Humility   NIV
1 Peter 5:5-6

In the same way, you who are younger, submit yourselves to your elders. All of you, clothe yourselves with humility toward one another, because, "God opposes the proud but shows favor to the humble." Humble yourselves, therefore, under God's mighty hand, that he may lift you up in due time.

1 Peter 5:5-6

E-4   *Grow in Christlikeness*

Purity   NIV
Ephesians 5:3

But among you there must not be even a hint of sexual immorality, or of any kind of impurity, or of greed, because these are improper for God's holy people.

Ephesians 5:3

E-5   *Grow in Christlikeness*

Purity   NIV
1 Peter 2:11

Dear friends, I urge you, as foreigners and exiles, to abstain from sinful desires, which wage war against your soul.

1 Peter 2:11

E-6   *Grow in Christlikeness*

Honesty   NIV
Leviticus 19:11

Do not steal. Do not lie. Do not deceive one another.

Leviticus 19:11

E-7   *Grow in Christlikeness*

Honesty   NIV
Acts 24:16

So I strive always to keep my conscience clear before God and man.

Acts 24:16

E-8   *Grow in Christlikeness*

Love   MSG

John 13:34-35

Let me give you a new command: Love one another. In the same way I loved you, you love one another. This is how everyone will recognize that you are my disciples — when they see the love you have for each other.

John 13:34-35

E-1   Grow in Christlikeness

Love   MSG

1 John 3:18

My dear children, let's not just talk about love; let's practice real love.

1 John 3:18

E-2   Grow in Christlikeness

Humility   MSG

Philippians 2:3-4

Don't push your way to the front; don't sweet-talk your way to the top. Put yourself aside, and help others get ahead. Don't be obsessed with getting your own advantage. Forget yourselves long enough to lend a helping hand.

Philippians 2:3-4

E-3   Grow in Christlikeness

Humility   MSG

1 Peter 5:5-6

And you who are younger must follow your leaders. But all of you, leaders and followers alike, are to be down to earth with each other, for God has had it with the proud, but takes delight in just plain people. So be content with who you are, and don't put on airs. God's strong hand is on you; he'll promote you at the right time.

1 Peter 5:5-6

E-4   Grow in Christlikeness

Purity   MSG

Ephesians 5:3

Don't allow love to turn into lust, setting off a downhill slide into sexual promiscuity, filthy practices, or bullying greed.

Ephesians 5:3

E-5   Grow in Christlikeness

Purity   MSG

1 Peter 2:11

Friends, this world is not your home, so don't make yourselves cozy in it. Don't indulge your ego at the expense of your soul.

1 Peter 2:11

E-6   Grow in Christlikeness

Honesty   MSG

Leviticus 19:11

Don't steal. Don't lie. Don't deceive anyone.

Leviticus 19:11

E-7   Grow in Christlikeness

Honesty   MSG

Acts 24:16

Believe me, I do my level best to keep a clear conscience before God and my neighbors in everything I do.

Acts 24:16

E-8   Grow in Christlikeness

E. Grow in Christlikeness

E. Grow in Christlikeness

Love   NASB
John 13:34-35

A new commandment I give to you, that you love one another, even as I have loved you, that you also love one another. By this all men will know that you are My disciples, if you have love for one another.

John 13:34-35

E-1   Grow in Christlikeness

Love   NASB
1 John 3:18

Little children, let us not love with word or with tongue, but in deed and truth.

1 John 3:18

E-2   Grow in Christlikeness

Humility   NASB
Philippians 2:3-4

Do nothing from selfishness or empty conceit, but with humility of mind regard one another as more important than yourselves; do not merely look out for your own personal interests, but also for the interests of others.

Philippians 2:3-4

E-3   Grow in Christlikeness

Humility   NASB
1 Peter 5:5-6

You younger men, likewise, be subject to your elders; and all of you, clothe yourselves with humility toward one another, for God is opposed to the proud, but gives grace to the humble. Therefore humble yourselves under the mighty hand of God, that He may exalt you at the proper time.

1 Peter 5:5-6

E-4   Grow in Christlikeness

Purity   NASB
Ephesians 5:3

But immorality or any impurity or greed must not even be named among you, as is proper among saints.

Ephesians 5:3

E-5   Grow in Christlikeness

Purity   NASB
1 Peter 2:11

Beloved, I urge you as aliens and strangers to abstain from fleshly lusts which wage war against the soul.

1 Peter 2:11

E-6   Grow in Christlikeness

Honesty   NASB
Leviticus 19:11

You shall not steal, nor deal falsely, nor lie to one another.

Leviticus 19:11

E-7   Grow in Christlikeness

Honesty   NASB
Acts 24:16

In view of this, I also do my best to maintain always a blameless conscience both before God and before men.

Acts 24:16

E-8   Grow in Christlikeness

E. Grow in Christlikeness

E. Grow in Christlikeness

Love NKJV

1 John 3:18

My little children, let us not love in word or in tongue, but in deed and in truth.

1 John 3:18

E-2   Grow in Christlikeness

Love NKJV

John 13:34-35

A new commandment I give to you, that you love one another; as I have loved you, that you also love one another. By this all will know that you are My disciples, if you have love for one another.

John 13:34-35

E-1   Grow in Christlikeness

Humility NKJV

1 Peter 5:5-6

Likewise you younger people, submit yourselves to your elders. Yes, all of you be submissive to one another, and be clothed with humility, for "God resists the proud, but gives grace to the humble." Therefore humble yourselves under the mighty hand of God, that He may exalt you in due time.

1 Peter 5:5-6

E-4   Grow in Christlikeness

Humility NKJV

Philippians 2:3-4

Let nothing be done through selfish ambition or conceit, but in lowliness of mind let each esteem others better than himself. Let each of you look out not only for his own interests, but also for the interests of others.

Philippians 2:3-4

E-3   Grow in Christlikeness

Purity NKJV

1 Peter 2:11

Beloved, I beg you as sojourners and pilgrims, abstain from fleshly lusts which war against the soul.

1 Peter 2:11

E-6   Grow in Christlikeness

Purity NKJV

Ephesians 5:3

But fornication and all uncleanness or covetousness, let it not even be named among you, as is fitting for saints.

Ephesians 5:3

E-5   Grow in Christlikeness

Honesty NKJV

Acts 24:16

This being so, I myself always strive to have a conscience without offense toward God and men.

Acts 24:16

E-8   Grow in Christlikeness

Honesty NKJV

Leviticus 19:11

You shall not steal, nor deal falsely, nor lie to one another.

Leviticus 19:11

E-7   Grow in Christlikeness

E. Grow in Christlikeness

E. Grow in Christlikeness

Love ESV

John 13:34-35

A new commandment I give to you, that you love one another: just as I have loved you, you also are to love one another. By this all people will know that you are my disciples, if you have love for one another.

John 13:34-35

E-1 Grow in Christlikeness

Love ESV

1 John 3:18

Little children, let us not love in word or talk but in deed and in truth.

1 John 3:18

E-2 Grow in Christlikeness

Humility ESV

Philippians 2:3-4

Do nothing from rivalry or conceit, but in humility count others more significant than yourselves. Let each of you look not only to his own interests, but also to the interests of others.

Philippians 2:3-4

E-3 Grow in Christlikeness

Humility ESV

1 Peter 5:5-6

Likewise, you who are younger, be subject to the elders. Clothe yourselves, all of you, with humility toward one another, for "God opposes the proud but gives grace to the humble." Humble yourselves, therefore, under the mighty hand of God so that at the proper time he may exalt you.

1 Peter 5:5-6

E-4 Grow in Christlikeness

Purity ESV

Ephesians 5:3

But sexual immorality and all impurity or covetousness must not even be named among you, as is proper among saints.

Ephesians 5:3

E-5 Grow in Christlikeness

Purity ESV

1 Peter 2:11

Beloved, I urge you as sojourners and exiles to abstain from the passions of the flesh, which wage war against your soul.

1 Peter 2:11

E-6 Grow in Christlikeness

Honesty ESV

Leviticus 19:11

You shall not steal; you shall not deal falsely; you shall not lie to one another.

Leviticus 19:11

E-7 Grow in Christlikeness

Honesty ESV

Acts 24:16

So I always take pains to have a clear conscience toward both God and man.

Acts 24:16

E-8 Grow in Christlikeness

Love KJV
1 John 3:18

My little children, let us not love in word, neither in tongue; but in deed and in truth.

1 John 3:18

E-2   Grow in Christlikeness

Love KJV
John 13:34-35

A new commandment I give unto you, That ye love one another; as I have loved you, that ye also love one another. By this shall all men know that ye are my disciples, if ye have love one to another.

John 13:34-35

E-1   Grow in Christlikeness

Humility KJV
1 Peter 5:5-6

Likewise, ye younger, submit yourselves unto the elder. Yea, all of you be subject one to another, and be clothed with humility: for God resisteth the proud, and giveth grace to the humble. Humble yourselves therefore under the mighty hand of God, that he may exalt you in due time.

1 Peter 5:5-6

E-4   Grow in Christlikeness

Humility KJV
Philippians 2:3-4

Let nothing be done through strife or vainglory; but in lowliness of mind let each esteem others better than themselves. Look not every man on his own things, but every man also on the things of others.

Philippians 2:3-4

E-3   Grow in Christlikeness

Purity KJV
1 Peter 2:11

Dearly beloved, I beseech you as strangers and pilgrims, abstain from fleshly lusts, which war against the soul.

1 Peter 2:11

E-6   Grow in Christlikeness

Purity KJV
Ephesians 5:3

But fornication, and all uncleanness, or covetousness, let it not be once named among you, as becometh saints.

Ephesians 5:3

E-5   Grow in Christlikeness

Honesty KJV
Acts 24:16

And herein do I exercise myself, to have always a conscience void of offense toward God, and toward men.

Acts 24:16

E-8   Grow in Christlikeness

Honesty KJV
Leviticus 19:11

Ye shall not steal, neither deal falsely, neither lie one to another.

Leviticus 19:11

E-7   Grow in Christlikeness

E. Grow in Christlikeness

E. Grow in Christlikeness

Love   NRSV

John 13:34-35

I give you a new commandment, that you love one another. Just as I have loved you, you also should love one another. By this everyone will know that you are my disciples, if you have love for one another.

John 13:34-35

E-1   Grow in Christlikeness

Love   NRSV

1 John 3:18

Little children, let us love, not in word or speech, but in truth and action.

1 John 3:18

E-2   Grow in Christlikeness

Humility   NRSV

Philippians 2:3-4

Do nothing from selfish ambition or conceit, but in humility regard others as better than yourselves. Let each of you look not to your own interests, but to the interests of others.

Philippians 2:3-4

E-3   Grow in Christlikeness

Humility   NRSV

1 Peter 5:5-6

In the same way, you who are younger must accept the authority of the elders. And all of you must clothe yourselves with humility in your dealings with one another, for "God opposes the proud, but gives grace to the humble." Humble yourselves therefore under the mighty hand of God, so that he may exalt you in due time.

1 Peter 5:5-6

E-4   Grow in Christlikeness

Purity   NRSV

Ephesians 5:3

But fornication and impurity of any kind, or greed, must not even be mentioned among you, as is proper among saints.

Ephesians 5:3

E-5   Grow in Christlikeness

Purity   NRSV

1 Peter 2:11

Beloved, I urge you as aliens and exiles to abstain from the desires of the flesh that wage war against the soul.

1 Peter 2:11

E-6   Grow in Christlikeness

Honesty   NRSV

Leviticus 19:11

You shall not steal; you shall not deal falsely; and you shall not lie to one another.

Leviticus 19:11

E-7   Grow in Christlikeness

Honesty   NRSV

Acts 24:16

Therefore I do my best always to have a clear conscience toward God and all people.

Acts 24:16

E-8   Grow in Christlikeness

E. Grow in Christlikeness

E. Grow in Christlikeness

Love NLT

1 John 3:18

Dear children, let us stop just saying we love each other; let us really show it by our actions.

1 John 3:18

Love NLT

John 13:34-35

So now I am giving you a new commandment: Love each other. Just as I have loved you, you should love each other. Your love for one another will prove to the world that you are my disciples.

John 13:34-35

Humility NLT

1 Peter 5:5-6

You younger men, accept the authority of the elders. And all of you, serve each other in humility, for "God sets himself against the proud, but he shows favor to the humble." So humble yourselves under the mighty power of God, and in his good time he will honor you.

1 Peter 5:5-6

Humility NLT

Philippians 2:3-4

Don't be selfish; don't live to make a good impression on others. Be humble, thinking of others as better than yourself. Don't think only about your own affairs, but be interested in others, too, and what they are doing.

Philippians 2:3-4

Purity NLT

1 Peter 2:11

Dear brothers and sisters, you are foreigners and aliens here. So I warn you to keep away from evil desires because they fight against your very souls.

1 Peter 2:11

Purity NLT

Ephesians 5:3

Let there be no sexual immorality, impurity, or greed among you. Such sins have no place among God's people.

Ephesians 5:3

Honesty NLT

Acts 24:16

Because of this, I always try to maintain a clear conscience before God and everyone else.

Acts 24:16

Honesty NLT

Leviticus 19:11

Do not steal. Do not cheat one another. Do not lie.

Leviticus 19:11

E. Grow in Christlikeness

E. Grow in Christlikeness

Faith

NIV

Hebrews 11:6

And without faith it is impossible to please God, because anyone who comes to him must believe that he exists and that he rewards those who earnestly seek him.

Hebrews 11:6

E-9   Grow in Christlikeness

Faith

NIV

Romans 4:20-21

Yet he did not waver through unbelief regarding the promise of God, but was strengthened in his faith and gave glory to God, being fully persuaded that God had power to do what he had promised.

Romans 4:20-21

E-10   Grow in Christlikeness

Good Works

NIV

Galatians 6:9-10

Let us not become weary in doing good, for at the proper time we will reap a harvest if we do not give up. Therefore, as we have opportunity, let us do good to all people, especially to those who belong to the family of believers.

Galatians 6:9-10

E-11   Grow in Christlikeness

Good Works

NIV

Matthew 5:16

In the same way, let your light shine before others, that they may see your good deeds and glorify your Father in heaven.

Matthew 5:16

E-12   Grow in Christlikeness

TOPICAL MEMORY SYSTEM

A. Live the New Life
Christ the Center — 2 Corinthians 5:17; Galatians 2:20
Obedience to Christ — Romans 12:1; John 14:21
God's Word — 2 Timothy 3:16; Joshua 1:8
Prayer — John 15:7; Philippians 4:6-7
Fellowship — 1 John 1:3; Hebrews 10:24-25
Witnessing — Matthew 4:19; Romans 1:16

B. Proclaim Christ
All Have Sinned — Romans 3:23; Isaiah 53:6
Sin's Penalty — Romans 6:23; Hebrews 9:27
Christ Paid the Penalty — Romans 5:8; 1 Peter 3:18
Salvation Not by Works — Ephesians 2:8-9; Titus 3:5
Must Receive Christ — John 1:12; Revelation 3:20
Assurance of Salvation — 1 John 5:13; John 5:24

C. Rely on God's Resources
His Spirit — 1 Corinthians 3:16; 1 Corinthians 2:12
His Strength — Isaiah 41:10; Philippians 4:13
His Faithfulness — Lamentations 3:22-23; Numbers 23:19
His Peace — Isaiah 26:3; 1 Peter 5:7
His Provision — Romans 8:32; Philippians 4:19
His Help in Temptation — Hebrews 2:18; Psalm 119:9, 11

D. Be Christ's Disciple
Put Christ First — Matthew 6:33; Luke 9:23
Separate from the World — 1 John 2:15-16; Romans 12:2
Be Steadfast — 1 Corinthians 15:58; Hebrews 12:3
Serve Others — Mark 10:45; 2 Corinthians 4:5
Give Generously — Proverbs 3:9-10; 2 Corinthians 9:6-7
Develop World Vision — Acts 1:8; Matthew 28:19-20

TOPICAL MEMORY SYSTEM (cont)

E. Grow in Christlikeness
Love — John 13:34-35; 1 John 3:18
Humility — Philippians 2:3-4; 1 Peter 5:5-6
Purity — Ephesians 5:3; 1 Peter 2:11
Honesty — Leviticus 19:11; Acts 24:16
Faith — Hebrews 11:6; Romans 4:20-21
Good Works — Galatians 6:9-10; Matthew 5:16

© The Navigators 1969, 1981, 2006

This Pack Belongs To

Name _____

Address _____

_____

Phone _____

If found, please return to above address.

E. Grow in Christlikeness

E. Grow in Christlikeness

Faith   MSG

Romans 4:20-21

He didn't tiptoe around God's promise asking cautiously skeptical questions. He plunged into the promise and came up strong, ready for God, sure that God would make good on what he had said.

Romans 4:20-21

E-10   Grow in Christlikeness

Faith   MSG

Hebrews 11:6

It's impossible to please God apart from faith. And why? Because anyone who wants to approach God must believe both that he exists *and* that he cares enough to respond to those who seek him.

Hebrews 11:6

E-9   Grow in Christlikeness

Good Works   MSG

Matthew 5:16

Now that I've put you there on a hilltop, on a light stand — shine! Keep open house; be generous with your lives. By opening up to others, you'll prompt people to open up with God, this generous Father in heaven.

Matthew 5:16

E-12   Grow in Christlikeness

Good Works   MSG

Galatians 6:9-10

So let's not allow ourselves to get fatigued doing good. At the right time we will harvest a good crop if we don't give up, or quit. Right now, therefore, every time we get the chance, let us work for the benefit of all, starting with the people closest to us in the community of faith.

Galatians 6:9-10

E-11   Grow in Christlikeness

E. Grow in Christlikeness

E. Grow in Christlikeness

Faith NASB

Hebrews 11:6

And without faith it is impossible to please Him, for he who comes to God must believe that He is and that He is a rewarder of those who seek Him.

Hebrews 11:6

E-9   Grow in Christlikeness

Faith NASB

Romans 4:20-21

Yet, with respect to the promise of God, he did not waver in unbelief but grew strong in faith, giving glory to God, and being fully assured that what God had promised, He was able also to perform.

Romans 4:20-21

E-10   Grow in Christlikeness

Good Works NASB

Galatians 6:9-10

Let us not lose heart in doing good, for in due time we will reap if we do not grow weary. So then, while we have opportunity, let us do good to all people, and especially to those who are of the household of the faith.

Galatians 6:9-10

E-11   Grow in Christlikeness

Good Works NASB

Matthew 5:16

Let your light shine before men in such a way that they may see your good works, and glorify your Father who is in heaven.

Matthew 5:16

E-12   Grow in Christlikeness

E. Grow in Christlikeness

E. Grow in Christlikeness

Faith NKJV

Romans 4:20-21

He did not waver at the promise of God through unbelief, but was strengthened in faith, giving glory to God, and being fully convinced that what He had promised He was also able to perform.

Romans 4:20-21

E-10   Grow in Christlikeness

Faith NKJV

Hebrews 11:6

But without faith it is impossible to please Him, for he who comes to God must believe that He is, and that He is a rewarder of those who diligently seek Him.

Hebrews 11:6

E-9   Grow In Christlikeness

Good Works NKJV

Matthew 5:16

Let your light so shine before men, that they may see your good works and glorify your Father in heaven.

Matthew 5:16

E-12   Grow in Christlikeness

Good Works NKJV

Galatians 6:9-10

And let us not grow weary while doing good, for in due season we shall reap if we do not lose heart. Therefore, as we have opportunity, let us do good to all, especially to those who are of the household of faith.

Galatians 6:9-10

E-11   Grow in Christlikeness

E. Grow in Christlikeness

E. Grow in Christlikeness

Faith   ESV
Hebrews 11:6

And without faith it is impossible to please him, for whoever would draw near to God must believe that he exists and that he rewards those who seek him.

Hebrews 11:6

E-9   Grow in Christlikeness

Faith   ESV
Romans 4:20-21

No distrust made him waver concerning the promise of God, but he grew strong in his faith as he gave glory to God, fully convinced that God was able to do what he had promised.

Romans 4:20-21

E-10   Grow in Christlikeness

Good Works   ESV
Galatians 6:9-10

And let us not grow weary of doing good, for in due season we will reap, if we do not give up. So then, as we have opportunity, let us do good to everyone, and especially to those who are of the household of faith.

Galatians 6:9-10

E-11   Grow in Christlikeness

Good Works   ESV
Matthew 5:16

In the same way, let your light shine before others, so that they may see your good works and give glory to your Father who is in heaven.

Matthew 5:16

E-12   Grow in Christlikeness

E. Grow in Christlikeness

E. Grow in Christlikeness

Faith   KJV

Romans 4:20-21

He staggered not at the promise of God through unbelief; but was strong in faith, giving glory to God; And being fully persuaded that, what he had promised, he was able also to perform.

Romans 4:20-21

E-10   Grow in Christlikeness

Faith   KJV

Hebrews 11:6

But without faith it is impossible to please him: for he that cometh to God must believe that he is, and that he is a rewarder of them that diligently seek him.

Hebrews 11:6

E-9   Grow in Christlikeness

Good Works   KJV

Matthew 5:16

Let your light so shine before men, that they may see your good works, and glorify your Father which is in heaven.

Matthew 5:16

E-12   Grow In Christlikeness

Good Works   KJV

Galatians 6:9-10

And let us not be weary in well doing: for in due season we shall reap, if we faint not. As we have therefore opportunity, let us do good unto all men, especially unto them who are of the household of faith.

Galatians 6:9-10

E-11   Grow in Christlikeness

E. Grow in Christlikeness

E. Grow in Christlikeness

Faith
NRSV

Hebrews 11:6

And without faith it is impossible to please God, for whoever would approach him must believe that he exists and that he rewards those who seek him.

Hebrews 11:6

E-9   Grow in Christlikeness

Faith
NRSV

Romans 4:20-21

No distrust made him waver concerning the promise of God, but he grew strong in his faith as he gave glory to God, being fully convinced that God was able to do what he had promised.

Romans 4:20-21

E-10   Grow in Christlikeness

Good Works
NRSV

Galatians 6:9-10

So let us not grow weary in doing what is right, for we will reap at harvest time, if we do not give up. So then, whenever we have an opportunity, let us work for the good of all, and especially for those of the family of faith.

Galatians 6:9-10

E-11   Grow In Christlikeness

Good Works
NRSV

Matthew 5:16

In the same way, let your light shine before others, so that they may see your good works and give glory to your Father in heaven.

Matthew 5:16

E-12   Grow in Christlikeness

E. Grow in Christlikeness

E. Grow in Christlikeness

Faith NLT

Romans 4:20-21

Abraham never wavered in believing God's promise. In fact, his faith grew stronger, and in this he brought glory to God. He was absolutely convinced that God was able to do anything he promised.

Romans 4:20-21

E-10   Grow in Christlikeness

Faith NLT

Hebrews 11:6

So, you see, it is impossible to please God without faith. Anyone who wants to come to him must believe that there is a God and that he rewards those who sincerely seek him.

Hebrews 11:6

E-9   Grow in Christlikeness

Good Works NLT

Matthew 5:16

In the same way, let your good deeds shine out for all to see, so that everyone will praise your heavenly Father.

Matthew 5:16

E-12   Grow in Christlikeness

Good Works NLT

Galatians 6:9-10

So don't get tired of doing what is good. Don't get discouraged and give up, for we will reap a harvest of blessing at the appropriate time. Whenever we have the opportunity, we should do good to everyone, especially to our Christian brothers and sisters.

Galatians 6:9-10

E-11   Grow In Christlikeness